ONE YEAR WITHOUT JONATHAN

One Year Without Jonathan

a journey through grief and healing

Karen L Swisher-McKee

ISBN-13: 9781537592121
ISBN-10: 1537592122

DEDICATION

To Jon, Jessica, and Jonathan

FORWARD

I DON'T EVEN KNOW how I'm going to write this. I'm not a writer. I just know the story needs to be written if not just for myself, then for Jonathan. When my son died I read approximately 50 books on grieving, self help, and spirituality. It really saved me. So, I'm putting forth my experiences for about one year after Jonathan died (funny thing I first typed "I died" Freudian slip?) so that maybe I can help people. Maybe I can help others know how to help grieving people. Maybe I can give people who just lost a loved one, especially a child, an idea of how they can survive the first year. Maybe I can help myself. It's a rough story. I'm not going to sugar coat it. I want you to know how hard it was to lose my son. Oh that first year was just so physically painful and life altering. I want you to know because I felt very misunderstood. Grief is a taboo subject. Suicide even more so. Guess what though, it happens every day and if it happened to you, you would want to be understood and supported. You would want to have hope that you could live your life again. You would want to know how to heal. So here it is, my life without Jonathan. The life of a mom without her son.

I already know what the reviews will be. I'm hallucinating….I'm not following the words in the bible… not deep enough…boring…but maybe ONE of you will love it and that's enough for me. I still need to write it though! I just sat down and let the words flow out of me, no editing. I thought maybe I would go back and change things or maybe put it in chapters. After taking some time to let my story gel, I decided not to edit it. I decided not to let others influence what I wrote or what I thought. This is raw and my authentic feelings as it was happening and I wasn't worrying about grammar as the words bled from my heart. Please note that there have been some very minor changes in details to protect privacy.

ONE YEAR WITHOUT JONATHAN, A JOURNEY THROUGH GRIEF

NOT IN A million years did I ever think I would come home and find you dead! How could such an ordinary life lead to this? I'm still in shock. A gunshot wound. You were life itself, always in action, wake boarding, skiing, shooting your sister with rubber bands. You were the most adventurous vital person I knew! I still don't understand. When I found you, the first memory that came back to me was of you when you were six going down a three story slide into the ocean in the dark. I could not put the image together with what I was seeing. I could not understand why this was happening, but it was.

It was November, 2014, living an active family life in suburban Detroit. I was a forty eight year old mother of two, working part time as a podiatrist. My husband worked in the automotive industry as a sales engineer. My husband and I did an adequate job of dividing up home responsibilities and the child rearing as we both worked. We were equals and respective of what each of us brought to the table. We had a well oiled system. He was the chef and grocery shopper. I was the activities director and the personal shopper. We made a wonderful team, honestly, he's my best friend. In my opinion we had created a dream life. We lived in a safe community with top public schools. The kids did not have any financial worries. We enriched their lives with robotic classes, had a garden at a community farm to learn about living green, got certified in SCUBA, learned to sail, took Tai Kwon Do, and the list goes on. We were very busy. We were focused on academics and being successful, but we tried to keep life balanced. We had a lot of fun too. Jonathan was the trickster of the family. When he was a baby, we would all be sitting in the living room playing and he would wait until I was distracted and slowly inch his way over to the hallway. When I would spot him and call his name he would crawl as fast as he could down the hall, laughing because he made me get up and chase him. He did this over and over. Jessica was the first child, a loving, cheerful, sunny girl and the responsible one. She and Jonathan were your typical siblings fighting like animals one second and the next second thick as thieves. One of our favorite things to do was to tell stories. The kids loved to sit around the table and listen to stories about our lives when we were younger. They liked me to make up stories about anything. All the time, it was, "Tell me a story Mom…". I used to make up stories about the Scooby Doo gang and make up my own villains when they were little. I didn't think I would ever be telling this story.

The kids grew up. Jonathan was in seventh grade and Jessica in her first year of high school. They had just finished their fall sports. Jessica got her varsity letter in swimming and Jonathan had finished football, one of the only seventh graders to start the games. We had a few down weeks before the next season's sports started and I was enjoying having them home after school for once! Normally I would pick them up from practice right before dinner, but now that sports were over they had some time alone after school. It was the first day without a babysitter waiting at home for them. They promised they were old enough to be at home alone after school until I got home from work. I had to agree that by twelve and fourteen they aught to be able to handle an hour alone. I specifically looked at Jonathan and asked him if he was sure he could behave for an hour and he confidently nodded his head yes. So I let the babysitter go.

If the story sounds boring so far, that's because life was uneventful. There were no dramatic situations leading up to his death. I can't even look back in hindsight and see any signs.

The day Jonathan died was a perfect clear and crisp fall day. I was giddy with excitement. We were finally moving into the dream house! All my hard work paying off. My husband, Jon, got his promotion that he deserved for years. I had adrenaline flowing through my body about my business. I was ready to kick some butt and expand it. I flew through the day. I saw all my patients on time. I remember joking with them and having fun. I just had this feeling that things were going to change, but I thought in a good way. We had two showings on our house and I was positive one of them would be a buyer. I looked up to the sun shining through the clouds and thought God was sending me a message. I felt like God was commanding my attention. I thought he was telling me how great my life was going to be. Unfortunately I was wrong. He was telling me I would need his support because you were already dead.

After I finished up with my patients I picked Jessica up from the gym, dropped her off at home and went to Jonathan's school for his conferences.

Well conferences went better than I thought they were, despite how I saw you struggle, the teachers I saw had only very good things to say about you. The one comment that sticks in my mind was, "confident". I bought two chocolate covered Rice Krispy treats for you and Jessica and ran home to share the good news with you. I stopped in front of the garage that didn't work and honked my horn. Usually you came right away and opened the door from inside for me. I honked again and no one came to the garage. So I went to the front door that was locked and I pounded on it. No one came to the door. The extra key was in the lock box and I finally opened the door myself. I had a smile on my face and was happy. You were doing good in school. You needed help in writing, but I was eager to help you.

I called your name. I went into your room. Where were you? Your backpack was in the hall. I asked Jessica where you were? She casually said she didn't know as she snacked and watched tv. Did you go for a bike ride? I called Jon. Did he know where you were? I was very confused, but still not too concerned. I opened the backdoor and saw you lying face down on the cement. I screamed your name and you didn't move. Were you playing a joke on me? Remember you used to hide from me and make me search for you when I came home? I ran over and shook you. Then I saw the blood. What happened? What happened? I felt for your pulse and there wasn't one. Who hurt you? I just started screaming for help. Jessica was screaming. I was shaking your body as if I could wake you up. The truth too painful to face yet, even though you did not have a pulse. Two neighbors, still unknown to me came to my backyard and called 911. Jon came running home and was bewildered. The cops came. The paramedics came. I can still see your body convulsing from the paddles. Lights were flashing. This is not happening! Chaos and questions. The cops were trying to ask me questions. How was he laying when you found him? Where were you? What time did you get home? All I wanted to do was to hold your hand and be with you, but I had to let the paramedics work on your body. As I sat there praying for a miracle, the devil whispered in my ear, an actual sinister voice in my ear, and said "You'll have more money now. You only have one to put through college." That voice haunts me to this day. I quickly shook that voice out of my ear and went back to praying.

They took you away to the hospital. As the gurney was lifted into the ambulance I saw you only had one shoe on and I wanted to put the other shoe on your foot. I didn't want you to leave without your shoe. We followed behind saying every prayer we knew of, but mostly just "Please. Please save him." We ran into the hospital, but you never made it. They told me you had been pronounced dead.

The light switch went out. I fell down a deep dark hole as if I could find you and bring you back. I felt like you were somewhere in the darkness. You weren't dead. If I could just find you in the darkness I could bring you back. But I couldn't find you. This is impossible. This is impossible. And then I landed hard breaking every bone in my body. I never wanted to come out. I didn't want to live either. I just wanted to stay in that dark hole. It's not as if I would actually kill myself, but I also did not want to be alive. I just did not want to exist.

We huddled together all night, holding each other in the darkness. Crying. Shaking. Despaired. Our bodies broken and our hearts filled with shattered glass, each breath caused pain to slice through my body. This was a surreal experience. Jonathan is gone. Jonathan is gone! Each minute was like an hour. Each hour like a day. The only word in my head was, "why?" Why did you do this? Why did this happen? Why wasn't I home? Why didn't anyone know?

Almost 2 years later we still don't know what happened to him to cause him to impulsively end his life. We don't even know if it was an accident. The police did an investigation at school. They interviewed his friends and the football team. They checked his computer and cell phone. Nothing. We looked through his back pack and books. Nothing. Nothing at all to tell us what happened. The weekend prior we had gone shopping and looked for new furniture for his room. He was going to decorate it in camo. We looked at the 4 wheelers and he asked could he get one if he got all As? I said yes and he shook his fist in the air and shouted "yes!". Some things happened to him that any regular 12 year old would go through. He had a detention. Someone wrote a mean comment on his Instagram. Someone called him a name. We talked about it. He seemed to let it roll off his shoulders. We talked about better ways of dealing with things. We were there for him, on his team. The morning he died, he said, "Love, you Mom." and I said, "Love you too, bud. Have a good day!" I asked him if he thought it was too cold for shorts and he laughed at me. My husband called him while he was walking home from school and said it was just a normal call. About ten minutes later he was dead. He had tried to call 911, but they didn't know where the call was coming from. They didn't have the technology to track cell phones.

So many what ifs. What if Jessica hadn't gone to the gym, she would have been home when he got home. What if I hadn't gone to conferences? I considered skipping them, but I thought Jonathan would be mad at me. What if the babysitter had gone into the house instead of picking the check up off the porch? What if my sister would have stopped and said hello instead of going to my Mom's? What if? The questions rattled endlessly through our heads, feelings of guilt and blame searing our insides. Eventually you have to forgive yourself. You can blame yourself forever, but then live in shackles and I know Jonathan would want us to not only live, but to thrive. However at this moment I hadn't come to that realization. I fully blamed myself.

We didn't sleep at all that night. It was really quite a night out of a horror movie. Early in the morning my sister walked in the room and said she had to tell me something! She's not the most religious person. The kind of person that went to Sunday school as a kid, but never went back. To say she was spiritual would even be stretching it. So, what she had to say somewhat surprised me. She said she had been awakened by a pounding headache and she thought, "Well that's weird. I never have headaches in the morning." Then she heard Jonathan's voice in her head telling her to "Tell my mom and dad and Jessica it's not their fault." I asked her to describe what she meant? How was she hearing his voice? She said she heard it just like he was sitting next to her talking. Her words were exactly what I needed to hear at that moment. Of course, that would be the only thought in all of our heads for a long time. I had been at conferences while you were laying on the cement dead. Jon called you just before you died…Jessica was inside just a few feet away from you and didn't see you lying there. Why weren't we there? Why didn't we know? But you said it wasn't our fault and you handed me a flashlight to see in the dark. I was still at the bottom of a dark hole, but at least I could see a few feet in front of my face. It wasn't complete darkness.

Maybe you are wondering why did I so easily accept that my sister heard my son's voice and accepted his statement that we were not at fault? Well I guess a part of me just wanted to believe that, but also, I had already had several experiences that had lead me to more or less believe in the afterlife, as had my immediate family.

I was home for Thanksgiving vacation my senior year of college. My grandmother who was 91 at that time did not get up to celebrate the holiday. She said she was too tired but thought she would feel better if she just rested. I also was sick. I had the stomach flu. The day after Thanksgiving we took my grandmother to the ER. She was essentially herself, just tired and nauseated. She was sitting in her chair talking and she thought I should go home and rest since I was sick also. My mom said she would call me when they were ready to come home. I fully expected her to get some medicine and she would promptly come home. When she said goodbye to me I had no fear it would be her last words to me. I went home and immediately fell asleep. At some point I was dreaming that my grandmother was floating up into the sky and she told me not to feel bad, that she was fine, and not to be guilty I wasn't with her at the hospital when she died. As I saw her in my dreams floating away, my mom called me and woke me up and told me my grandmother had passed away.

I really didn't know what to make of that dream, but it was unusual enough to make me pause and wonder. Had my grandmother entered my dreams to give me a message as a spirit? I didn't consider it too much. I was a busy college student and moved on very quickly. I just was happy that I had the dream. I found it comforting.

Fast forward to 2009, I had another experience concerning my grandmother. My grandmother had been an active member of the Daughter's of the American Revolution (DAR). We have an ancestry line leading back to Samuel Prescott, a doctor that finished Paul Revere's ride. My grandmother was very proud to be a DAR, but her grandchildren considered it antiquated and frivolous. For some reason, I woke up in the middle of the night and thought I had to join the DAR. I got online and filled out a form with as much information that I knew. I got a call from the organization about a week later that they had verified the information and all they needed was a copy of my birth certificate and a copy of my grandmother's death certificate. This put a damper on progress. I am notoriously lazy when it comes to finding things like this. I asked my mom if she had my grandmother's death certificate. My mom's feeble answer of, "It's somewhere…" left me very doubtful of it's existence. I knew that as busy as I was I would probably not find it or take the time to call the county to get a copy. I considered the lack of certificate a dead end for the moment.

About a week later, my daughter came into my room and asked me if she could look in my closet. My closet was jam packed with all sorts of old clothes, purses, books, letters I had accumulated since college. She went digging around and came out with an old purse. "What is this purse?", she asked me? It was my grandmothers and I had no idea how it got in my closet. I didn't even know it still existed. My daughter asked if she could look in it and then she pulled out a wallet. She looked in the wallet and asked me what this piece of paper was? I looked at it and almost fainted! It was my grandmother's death certificate! Needless to say I joined the DAR. This experience took me one step closer to believing in an afterlife and having loved ones looking over us. It was still a little hard to completely believe in that though.

Now, little unexplainable things were always happening, like noises, hearing an unusual song, lights going out. This was just the background of my life though and I would always laugh and say we had a ghost. It was really a joke to me though, not something that I really thought was plausible. The two experiences with my grandmother opened the door of possibilities, but not realities. However my grandmother knew she could connect with me. From wherever her energy was, she knew I was the one she could communicate with.

A few years after the death certificate was found, my grandmother's sister, Frieda, passed away. She had lived in New Mexico my whole life and so I didn't really know her. The few times I had met her, she struck me as a very strong, opinionated woman, but also kind and caring in her gruff way. She was an avid doll collector and had a room with every kind of doll you could imagine. As a young girl I was enthralled with this! I'm remembering that she had Donny and Marie Osmond dolls which I wanted to take out of the display and keep for myself. She also was a genealogist and we owe her for digging deep into our family's past and finding out so many interesting stories and connections. When she died, I had moments of sadness, knowing that we lost an original. There aren't too many Frieda's left in this world. Several weeks went by and I really did not think of her death too much. Life continued as usual.

One night I had a dream that I was dreaming, but then woke up in my grandmother's old house in New York. The house was completely empty, but I recognized the walls and floorboards. It was as if I had been beamed up like Scotty from Star Trek from my bed to her house in New York. It was instantaneous. I seemed like I was really in her house and this wasn't a dream. The front door opened and a beam of light entered the room that was so bright it was like pure gold. It was a light like none other I had seen and it radiated love and warmth. I was wondering what was going on when two silhouettes were seen at the door. It terrified me because they somehow reminded me of the girl from the movie, The Ring. In the movie her long hair is covering her face completely and as she walks forward you get the sense she is going to hurt you. I was initially scared, but as they walked toward me I saw that it was my grandmother and another woman and not girls from The Ring! I was so happy to see my grandmother and was astonished that I was seeing a ghost. She commented casually that yes, I was seeing a ghost, but it was not a concern and that wasn't the reason she was there. I asked her why then was she visiting me? She motioned to the other woman indicating that was her purpose. There was something about this woman I recognized, and I thought it was a relative, but I didn't know quite who it was. She looked annoyed at my confusion and I felt bad so I lied and said that of course I knew who she was.

We sat down and she gave me a little lecture on life. She told me to live my life with character and not to cut corners. If I never cheated or lied I would never have to worry about getting in trouble. Life would work out just fine. As we were talking I thought maybe she was related to my Dad and I said so. She got angry and said no! And poof it was over. I was awake in my bed. I kept wondering who was that in my dream? By this point I was pretty convinced my grandmother was an active spirit that could communicate with me, so I knew I had seen her, but who was it she wanted me to talk to. A few days later I saw my mom and she gave me the funeral program for Frieda. I looked at the picture and thought that's her! My grandmother wanted me to know she was with Frieda! I told my mom about it and she laughed. "I asked her to send us a sign, but I didn't know it would come so fast!". My mom had visited weeks before she died. My aunt had a terminal illness so my mom knew it was their last time together and she asked her to give us a sign. I hadn't recognized her because she appeared to me younger with slightly darker hair as she looked in the funeral program.

Even though I knew that energy or spirits existed after death, it gave me very little relief after Jonathan died. As I said before my heart was in a dark cave and it was very painful. That little light I had from my sister and Jonathan"s message wasn't much. It was only a tiny light in front of my face, illuminating nothing.

I walked through the day after he died in utter disbelief. It really was an effort to breath. I would find that after a time I would be forced to take a deep breath and I realized I was holding my breath. It's hard even now to tap into the emotions I had that day. I think I packed them up and put them someplace safe in my mind and I don't want to unpack them ever. I still had his blood on my hands and clothes and I couldn't bear to wash them. I remember holding my bloody hands to my cheeks and thinking this is all I have. It's all I had. We had to go to the funeral home and pick out his coffin. All I wanted was for him to be surrounded in nature. I wanted the funeral to be natural and personal. Which coffin did I like the funeral director asked? None! He was showing us different coffins as if they were used cars. Look at this special lining. Did we want a biodegradable one or a metal one? Did we want flowers on his coffin? Such crazy questions! I wanted to scream, " Does it really matter? He's dead!". I wanted to honor who he was as a person. We chose a simple wood one with some greenery on top that made me feel like he was in a forest. It was the hardest day. At the funeral home they gave me his personal affects, a necklace with a bullet on it that he wore often and he loved it. It seemed so inappropriate at the moment, but I wore it to feel closer to him. He also had a marble in his pocket. He always liked little things like lego figures and miniature tools. I still keep the marble with me.

We came home feeling like our bodies were inside out. If only grief looked as bad as it feels, then maybe people would understand. We got to the garage and that started another fit of tears. Jonathan was always the one to get out and open the door since the car opener didn't work. There was a certain trick to it, the electric opener would open it about an inch or two and then it would stop. If you could push it while it was in motion those two inches, the door might open with assistance. Otherwise we would have to go to the front door and go through the house and open it from the inside of the garage. Out of habit, we clicked on the opener and the door opened! That was so crazy! I know that was Jonathan helping us. As you read all these signs you might be thinking it's all coincidence, but when it happened to us, it's like we KNEW. Unbelievably the door worked the rest of the time we lived there and it had been broken for 2 years. I always wondered if the new owners had garage door problems after we left. The signs helped us to think his spirit was somewhere, but for myself that was only a grain of comfort. I was very greedy and needy of signs. I ask for them all the time!

Coming home after picking out his coffin, all I can say is that it was taking every cell in my body to keep moving, yet if I laid down the sight of his body was all that filled my mind. People thought I was doing ok because I was up talking to people and we were hanging out, but I was so far from ok. I just couldn't be alone or I would see him dead. I didn't know how long it would take to get that out of my mind. I look at pictures from that time and even a year after and my eyes are hollow and silent. A third minister from our church (the one we had not attended in 10 years) stopped by to see us. Say what you want about organized religion, but three ministers came straight over to our house when we needed them. He was and is the warmest kindest man and at that time he was the youth minister so he had an understanding of what a twelve year old boy is all about. He had a feeling that he knew Jonathan and that was comforting. Again, miraculously his words, gave me strength to make it a few more moments. He said he believed Jonathan was in heaven and that is all I wanted to hear. I know many people would think, if there was a heaven and God, why would he let him die? I had no analytic skills at that moment. If the pastor said he was in heaven, he was in heaven. I remember showing the pastor all the photos of Jonathan in Alaska and telling him about the trip the past summer. One day they caught the biggest silver salmon of the summer! I had never seen Jonathan happier.

Jonathan and his Dad took a fishing trip to Alaska. Jonathan had saved up money in a jar for souvenirs in Alaska. He bought a special knife for Alaska with all kinds of doodads on it. While in Alaska on the boat, he needed to go to the bathroom and the captain let him out on the mud lands. He told Jonathan to be careful because you can sink in the mud and your foot can break off your body when pulling it out. Apparently, he had a moment of difficulty getting out of the mud, but he did. He credited his Timberland boots for saving him. I got him a new pair once school started, but he didn't want them. He just wanted the trusty old ones. Oddly, I read in his fifth grade memory book almost a year after he died that he wrote, "I want to retire in Alaska, go fishing and hunting till I die. I want my ashes spread at my cabin in Alaska." I have no doubt he is there right now.

So far the message from Jonathan in my sister's head and pastor's reassurance that yes, Jonathan was in heaven were getting me through the day. However, we were still feeling like we wanted to pull the skin off our bodies. The pain for all of us was enormous. We still fell on the ground in wailing tears. It was overwhelming, this big, black deep hole left in our family. Thus began the messages from Jonathan.

My sister, Paula, had been driving around trying to think of what to do to help us. She wanted to get a book, but she didn't know where to go. She was in from another city. Her friend called to see how it was going and she told her she was looking for a book. The book she was looking for, was Heaven is for Real. Her friend told her to try Meijer's. My sister called the store and asked if they had it. The person at the store said, yes, they have it and she would hold it for my sister. The store clerk said to specifically ask for her. So, off Paula went to Meijer's. When she got there she went to the desk in the book section, but the clerk was busy with someone else. She waited a few minutes and then got impatient. Remember she was grieving too. Her nephew and her son's best friend had died. We were all in pain. So she went to look for the book herself, but couldn't find it and with a feeling of defeat, she went back to the cashier to wait. After a few minutes the cashier asked if she was Paula and she confirmed that. The cashier said she had a story to tell her.

Some years back, her mom was very sick with cancer and was fearful of death. She had all these people say she was going to heaven and it would be ok, but she didn't believe them. The cashier somewhat felt the way her mom did. She wanted to believe, but she didn't quite know how. A few months after her mom died she dreamt she was sitting on a piano stool with her mom and dad and they were playing the piano and singing a hymn. They knew all the words of every stanza. When she woke up she realized she never heard this song before. How could she know all the words to a song she didn't know? It felt like her mom was giving her a message that there was a heaven and she was there with her husband. Later, she would hear the song for the first time and wonder how she had known it? If she had ever heard the song at some point in her life, she certainly did not know every word and she couldn't recall that she ever had.

My sister felt like she gave her a message to pass on to me. One to reassure me. I was a tiny bit reassured, but not enough. I'm still working on it being enough!

So my sister gave me the book and I was trying to read it. You may be wondering how I could read a book a day after my son died, but I was really trying anything, and I still try everything, to try and have a glimmer of hope that somewhere my son existed. I should add here that Heaven is for Real was a very helpful book. I read and read spiritual books during the first year some not as good as others. This one is in the top ten.

My sister was in the dining room reading radiographs for her job on her computer. She came out to check on me and we were chatting a bit. Out of her periphery she saw the light form the chandelier in the dining room go on and off, on and off. She felt like maybe that was a signal to go back to work. I know you are thinking why would anyone think that, but you do. You kind of KNOW when things are signs. When she sat down, there was a pop up screen on her computer with a quote from George S. Patton, "It is foolish and wrong to mourn the men who died. Rather we should thank God that such men lived." Another message from Jonathan! And such a good one too because all I had been able to think of was what he missed out on dying at 12. I wish

I would have told him how handsome he was. I wish I would have told him that someday a girl would fall in love with his beautiful blue eyes. Instead I was told by the quote to focus on how much we had shared in his 12 years and to consider his 12 years a gift. Honestly I don't know how many times I thought about the fact that I almost didn't have him. I had had a miscarriage right before I got pregnant with him and I always wondered what if I had had that child instead? So he was my gift for 12 years. And as a side note, he was obsessed with the army and Patton. I always thought it was so odd that he could watch old documentaries. He loved them. And he wanted to be in the army, in fact I had a deep fear I would lose him to war. He was very patriotic. He wanted to protect our country.

And so another sleepless night, our minds filled with only these thoughts, "I miss you. I love you. Why? I love you. I love you. Why? Why? Where are you? I miss you..." all night long. Perhaps we slept for an hour, only to awaken to a nightmare. This morning my sister, Valerie had another message for me. I had been saying over and over, "what am I going to do?" and Valerie said she had the answer for me. She had awoken with Jonathan's voice in her head to "tell my mom she needs to take care of Dad and Jessica!". Ok. I have a purpose. I guess I can't stay in this dark hole forever, I must take care of my family. So at this point I had a flashlight and now I was given a ladder to climb out of the hole. I didn't climb out, but I knew I had to at some point.

How does one hear a voice in your head? You know how you "hear" your thoughts in your head or you have a conversation in your head thinking about what you might say to someone? Well, it's not like that. It's like a real voice. A few times I wake up and it's a whisper. One time I heard my name and it was like someone yelling at me to get my attention. Does this make me schizophrenic? I hear voices? Well honestly if it happened more than a few times I would think I was. If you read a lot of the books about mediums they all say they feel a little crazy when it happens to them. For myself it was always just matter of fact. This happened and I responded to it and it helped me. Is it some part of your subconscious connecting with your conscious brain? I really couldn't say for sure. I've read so much about it though that I feel like there are enough people verifying my opinion that energy or spirits can speak to you.

That day my whole family met at the funeral home for a private viewing. You were so handsome. Jessica noticed that your hair had never been softer. I was so sad you were wearing your outfit I had bought for Christmas and we put your trusted Timberlands on your feet. I wish they had saved you this time. We all put a letter, a photo, a stuffed animal in your casket. We put a few of your precious coins in too. I remembered all those afternoons in the coin shop how you agonized over which one to get and relished talking to the owner about different coins. To say that was a difficult moment would be like saying Minnesota in the winter is cold, but lovely to see you one last time and kiss your forehead. We all felt like you were there. The candles were flickering and whether it was our imagination we chose to think it was you. My brother Eric, joked that if you were there to give us a sign. If someone stubbed his toe later we would know you were there. That gave us a good chuckle, but oddly enough, on the way out of the funeral home his son stubbed his toe so badly his nail partially fell off!

We had a few friends and family at our house and it had a subdued party atmosphere. All the boy cousins were roughing about and it broke my heart you were not there with them. All the boys, all 7 of them, were so close that they thought of each other as brothers not cousins. Thinking of all your adventures, ice fishing, snowmobiling on Spider Lake and almost running down a shanty, pretending to be Power Rangers, playing xbox, you were always in the thick of it. I was comforted by my family, but there was such an obvious hole where you should have been and it hurt. I still cannot believe you are not here.

Because of the Patton quote that popped up on Paula's computer, we felt compelled to watch the movie Patton. It might have been silly, but we thought maybe there was a hidden message in it. I'm not sure about a hidden message, but what I did find out is that Patton was a very driven successful commander. Unfortunately he was often misunderstood because he was trying to inspire the soldiers and toughen them up, but his words were sometimes seen as vulgar. I could identify that sometimes people thought Jonathan was a crazy wild boy, but I knew him to have a heart of gold. He felt things very deeply and was sensitive. The funny thing is there have been several other Patton moments. I was scrolling through my Facebook feed and a suggested article was a trip to visit Patton's grave. Weird! Another time there was a suggested post where there were pictures of pets after their owners died and there was one of Patton's dog. And then there was that movie that I randomly watched on you tube with Jack Wild in it. They were walking down the streets of London and there on a street corner was a huge poster advertising the movie Patton. There were so many more. It seemed like Patton was everywhere.

Another sleepless night of agony. Again my thoughts were only how much I missed him. Sleep, usually a pleasant respite, was like a Tim Burton movie for us, dark shadows and craggy trees, ghostly thoughts with scarecrow like bodies, guilt, blame, anger, sadness. I'm not sure if I'll ever divulge who this person is, but I had very visual thoughts of taking a baseball bat to the head of the person I blame. By this time it was our third sleepless night without food and we were exhausted but still only slept a few minutes.

The next day we were busy with arrangements. My family took care of every iota of the funeral. If they had not done it, there wouldn't have been one. We were absolutely not capable. They put together three trifold poster boards of pictures. They had to compile all of them off Facebook and phone cameras and get them developed and mounted. Looking at them it was just unbelievable he was dead. There he was scuba diving in the ocean. There he was hugging his sister. There he was tubing down a hill as fast as he could. His life was so full. I tried so hard to give him the adventures he craved. He wanted to fly. Life in this millennium was so different from mine. There were too many restrictions for him. He would have done so much better in the 70s where it was common for boys to ride around on their bikes carrying a bb gun. He was all boy. In this world of feminization of boys, he had a hard time fitting in. I realized all this while he was living and I gave him all kinds of opportunities to explore and feel free, but there were not enough. He wanted to feel like that all the time.

The dreadful day was here. His funeral. How I would even stand up? I didn't know. I had barely spoken more than a few sentences in the last few days. How would I greet people? How would I not dissolve into a puddle of tears? What would I say? I had no idea what I would wear. I just pulled out the first outfit I saw in my closet. I took my first shower and was saddened to wash his blood off my hand. No more life. I broke down on the floor of the shower. Why is this happening to me? I had no brain what so ever. I think I set my phone down 10 times and forgot where I put it. I wanted to wear your bullet necklace because it was yours, but again wondered about the appropriateness. I was literally running around the house with my proverbial head cut off, thinking about what jewelry to wear, who is driving with who, what time do we need to be at the church, where is my diet coke? I looked into my jewelry box and there it was. Something to ground me.

That past spring break we took our kids, their cousin Jenna, and Jonathan's best friend, TJ, to Cabo San Lucas. It was absolute perfection. We laughed so much. All the kids got along so well and they were old enough to be on their own a bit, while Jon and I relaxed and drank mojitos. The boys ate cream puffs all night. They went deep sea fishing and had a seal jump in their boat, which amazed them. They went parasailing, rode the waves, ate lobster, and the list goes on. One day we were at a farm that had a restaurant and a few stores there. We were in a jewelry store and a necklace struck my eye. I loved it. I'm not really a jewelry person, and I never spent that kind of money on myself so I did not even consider buying it, but Jonathan wanted me to get it. It was a coral cross on a gold chain. We stood there arguing over it. Jonathan would tell me to buy it and I would say it's too much. Jonathan went to get my husband and he wanted Jon to get it for me. Jon asked how much I liked it and I said I liked it so much I would wear it every day. He bought it! Jonathan was very proud of himself.

As life would have it, I didn't wear it every day. I didn't think it matched my outfits or sometimes. many times, I felt like it was too fancy for my mom yoga pants and sweatshirts. And then I lost it! I searched the house everywhere. I looked in my jewelry box at least 10 times. I thought it would turn up, but after cleaning the house from top to bottom while we were moving, I still hadn't found it and I just considered it lost forever. The kids were really mad at me! I was supposed to wear it every day! They felt like I disrespected them. So, on the day of his funeral when I was running around like a robot with a malfunctioning battery, I opened my jewelry box and there was the cross necklace right on top. How perfect was that? I had a part of him with me and a cross was much better than a bullet to wear to church! And yes, I wear it all the time now. Love you Jonathan!

We had the viewing first. The casket was closed, but we had all his pictures out and his memorabilia, like his skis and Tai Kwon Do outfit. That is pretty much a blur to me. There were so many people that came up and said their condolences, but I have no idea what I said. I was just struck by the amount of people who were there. This is not something we had ever ever planned for. You have no idea what to say to people. I am sure people didn't know what to say to me. The truth would be too horrific. Apparently there were a few people trying to find out what happened and asked my sister about it. Please note, I respectfully state that is not cool. Personally, if you are ever wondering whether you should go to a funeral, the answer is probably yes. I thought I wanted it to be completely private, but I realized so many people were grieving too. So many people wanted to pay their respects. As it turned out, it didn't matter that they weren't my close friends or family. The fact they were there for me was enough.

The funeral service was perfection. That one hour that we honored him was so special to me. I wished the actual funeral would go on forever. Please remember him! Think of all the funny things he did! Remember his pranks! Remember how much fun swim practice was with him! Remember him! Keep him in your heart forever.

We started the funeral with Madison's Rising rock version of the Star Spangled Banner. He would have wanted something like that. A few months later when I went to the cemetery to visit his grave that song would start playing on my phone all by itself as I drove in. Three of his cousins draped a flag over his casket. His Instagram bio stated, "America, that is all I have to say." Where this patriotism came from, I'm not sure. I would say my husband and I have a healthy dose of pride in our country, but it's not something we really talk about. Jonathan was the one to shake a veteran's hand. He loved the fourth of July, not just the fireworks, but to honor our freedom. However, I am sure my family, especially the kids remember one Fourth of July they sang a song about Jonathan and fireworks, "Give Jonathan his fireworks. Give Jonathan his fireworks. They go off. In his pants. Give Jonathan his fireworks…". Oh they thought that was funny!

After a few basic prayers, we played the song "It's My Life", by Bon Jovi. Jonathan was funny about music. He liked it all from Jazz to Adele to Bon Jovi to Lincoln Park to Katy Perry. I particularly liked these words from the song, "It's my life it's now or never. I ain't gonna live forever. I'm just going to live the way I live." Such true words for him. He was himself every second of the day. He wore pink socks with a camouflage jacket. He said what was on his mind. He was unique and had such a great sense of humor. The way he looked at life was refreshing. He continuously made comments that made me think, huh, you're right I never thought of it that way. I remember when he was about two years old and he couldn't quite reach his doorknob, he hooked a candy cane on it so he had a little handle. I also was thinking of how when he started to ski, he had only had a few lessons and he was decent, but his best friend had skied for years and was very good. His friend, TJ, said he would teach him how to ski and took him down a black diamond hill! And he did it! It's a good thing I didn't know about it at the time. Sometimes I think he knew he'd have to jam it all in. He'd have to do the black diamond before he was ready because he wouldn't have another chance. I do believe in eternal life, but we only get one chance to enjoy the physical life. And that is a constant reminder for me also. I try to live by Bon Jovi's words also because I am even more so conscious of how precious this life is. As time goes on I realize that in death we are given gifts. Jonathan gave me the gift of living in the present and not worrying about the future so much. I have always been a worry wort about everything, especially money and having enough. When you lose a life it's so obvious how meaningless it all is.

So the minister gave his (speech). It was very warm and personal. You'd have thought the two of them were best buds, but in fact they had never met. He got a very good sense of Jonathan from talking to our family and looking at his pictures. He recounted a classic story of Jonathan that had taken place many years ago on that same altar.

Jonathan was baptized at the First Methodist Church of Birmingham when he was four years old. The minister at that time asked him if he knew why he was there and Jonathan answered, "You're going to take the devil out of me." That got a good laugh from the pews. No, the minister explained to him why he was there and a simple explanation of what baptism meant. When it was finished, Jonathan told the minister that it didn't work, "I still have the devil in me." Now he didn't mean the actual devil. He meant that spark of life that made him get into mischief, and mischief was his middle name. He was right! The baptism did nothing to stop his mischief.

The minister read from a book, I Love you This Much, a story about a mama bear and her cub and how they go through the day together learning how wide and long and high love is between two people and the love of God. It was very touching and true. I was thinking of how I would tell the kids that if something happened to them I would cry every day for the rest of my life. So far, that is true.

My two sisters and brother gave eulogies. It was so hard for them. I'm so proud of the words and stories that they shared with people that may not have known him well. They were inspiring and positive. Let us learn from this tragedy. Let us be better people. Let us honor the way he lived his life and be as adventurous and full of life as he was.

We finished the funeral with the song, Angel by Sarah Mclachlan, "You're in the arms of an angel. May you find some comfort here." I am not joking that that song comes on every single day in my car. I have my cell phone on shuffle and most of the time the volume is off and I will casually glance at the middle console and there I see that Angel is playing, every single day. I might be having a bad moment and I look up and the song is playing. It's the most bizarre thing, but it always makes me smile.

We had people over at our house and by this time, I was shaking inside. I was standing and looking normal on the outside, but on the inside I was breaking down. Jon and I went to lay down, but we could still hear everyone talking. "My son plays hockey." "My son plays lacrosse." "My son is looking at this college." "My son is being recruited by professional teams." My son is dead. Another mostly sleepless night.

In the morning Jessica told us about an odd dream she had that past night. She dreamt that Jonathan had legs made out of some type of musical instruments sort of like saxophones. He was talking to a classmate. The classmate asked where he was going? Jonathan pointed to a door. The classmate asked why? Jonathan said not to worry it's fine and he walked out the door.

We never really know what the dreams mean or if they are real, but they sure offer comfort in those painful painful moments. The day after the funeral we didn't get out of bed once, not all day.

People comment and wonder what it was like? They know it's a very sad thing to lose a child. They can feel a horrible sinking feeling if they think about it. For me, like I said I first felt like I was in a dark cave and just did not want to live. I felt like I was dead. But the dreams, messages, the funeral, family, got me out of the cave at least for the moment, but not into the light. For a very, very long time I was fifty feet underwater my body shackled to weights. I was only ever so slightly aware of the world around me. There was a vague glimmer of a light above me and voices were muffled. These were the calm moments. The bad times felt like I was again, under water, but in addition someone was stabbing me over and over in the heart. That probably sounds cliche, but that is the way it felt, on and off all day. This is how I felt every day for a year and a half and I wondered if I would ever get better? Imagine trying to get into your car with chains and weights on your body. The effort it took just to get out of bed was unreal for me. I can't say that for one moment I felt happy. There were moments I felt better. There were things that put a smile on my face, but actual happiness was not even possible. As I write this today, almost 2 years later, I have felt almost happy at times. It is getting more frequent.

I was told by that voice in my sister's head to take care of my family. So, like a soldier the next day I went back to work. Jon went back to work and Jessica went back to school. I didn't really know how I was going to do this because I was crying non stop, but I only had three patients and previously would have been the easiest day so I thought I would be ok. I didn't realize that this was going to be as hard as it was. Not only was I crying, but I was dragging around those chains of guilt, pain, and blame. I pulled into the gas station because I couldn't see the road from my tears and wondered how I would ever pull it together. I went into the gas station to get something to drink and the song Hey Jude by the Beatles was on. "Take a sad song and make it better. Remember to let her into your heart, then you will start to make it better." These are the kinds of things that kept me from falling back into the black hole, little messages, hugs, small things. Ok so I have the saddest song of all but I can make it better. I can do this.

My first patient was practically unresponsive so thankfully for myself she did not notice the state I was in. As I was taking off her socks, I could hear her TV in the other room playing a song. It sounded familiar. What was that song? Oh yes! It was a song we sang in college when we were drunk, walking home from the bar. It was an obscure movie from the 50s or 60s maybe. I have no idea what the name of the movie is. But the words we sang were, "Baby. Baby. I just want to take you where I'm going. Baby. Baby. I just want to make you mine." My friend had been watching the movie late at night with her boyfriend and for some reason we thought it was hilarious! And here I was in a patients room and the movie was on the TV and it made me smile. My first smile, although I did not feel that smile in my heart I did register that I was capable of smiling. So I went about my business finishing up with the patient, routine foot care. As I was leaving the patient looked up at me and said, "Take good care of your family." That was kind of eery because that is the only thing she said to me and that was the only reason I was there, to take care of my family.

After I saw the patient I was so exhausted I had to sit down and rest. Keep in mind less than a week ago I had skipped through a day, laughing and connecting with my patients. I was ready to expand my business. Now, seeing one patient felt like I had seen one hundred. I sat for about 20 minutes when I finally got the ability to get up. My next patient also was not in the best mental state so also did not really notice that I was crying and wiping my tears away. I glanced to a night light (not sure why it caught my eye) and the light went off, on, off, on, off, on, in a steady pace not a flicker. It made my heart skip a beat because I felt like it was Jonathan saying he was there with me and it was going to be ok.

I finished my last patient and was so incredibly happy to be heading home. I just wanted to go to bed! About ten minutes before I got home I received a call from a mom whose son went to school with mine. I thought she was going to tell me how sorry she was and I almost didn't answer it, but I did and then she told me that I should call an ambulance because she was at my house and my mom had taken a fall and she could see in the window that her head was bleeding. My heart practically jumped out of my body! I called the ambulance and I raced home. I was praying all the while. This couldn't happen again! Yet I knew it could. I knew elderly couples that died a few days apart and their families had to deal with dual funerals. Please no!

I ran into the house and my mom was sitting up with a bandage wrapped around her head. The paramedics had to force her to go to the hospital where she got 12 staples! Oh boy. Thus began a month long stay at our house where she slept in Jonathan's room. She had many adventures in that room. His light would flicker. A picture frame suddenly fell over. She thought she heard him calling her name every morning when she woke up. You know, I don't know how to explain it and unfortunately something you have to experience, but when the lights flicker it really seemed like it was him! I also felt like I could connect with him in his room. After my mom left I would go into his room to journal and I would write him a letter and then I would write his response. His answers just flowed from me. I really can't say for sure if I was channeling him, but it felt like I was.

Dear Jonathan,

I so miss you! I can't tell you how much I miss your jokes. I feel so bad I wasn't here. I don't know how to get over this. Everyday feels like an eternity without you. Wherever you are I pray you are ok. Love you so much!

Mom

Dear Mom,

I miss you so much too! But I'm still here. I am still riding to school with Jessica. I'm watching tv with you. I know you can't see me, but you can feel me. I will explain to you one day what happened, but until then you just have to live your life. Love you too Mom!

Jonathan

Dear Jonathan,

Everyday is so hard for me. I can't imagine what happened. I so want to hug you and kiss you and make it all better. I know it was a huge mistake. You didn't know what would happen. I don't know why this is God's plan? It feels so unfair. Though I imagine you wake boarding through heaven and hanging out with Happy Pappy. I know they will love you and take care of you until we meet again. Love you so much!

Mom

Dear Mom,

I'm so sorry. I didn't mean to hurt you. Heaven is perfect and amazing, but I have work to do here. I am working on my soul. I still have to live on with knowing how much I hurt you and I'm so sorry.

Jonathan

Dear Jonathan,

I am really trying to embrace this, to be happy for the man that lived and to celebrate your 12 years. And I do. And I have taken that leap of faith and I am trusting that you are playing to your hearts content. But my heart aches to touch you, to hear your laugh. I just still miss you so much! My heart is so heavy. So many good memories, but they make me cry. I am putting one foot in front of the next, but it is very hard. My feet are like blocks of cement. You were so beautiful. So beautiful. Love you!

Mom

Dear Mom,

You are just going to have to let all the questions go. I know it's hard, but you will never have the answer you want. Every time you put a thought in your head of what happened that day, you are wrong. I will tell you someday. Keep remembering me. Write down all our memories. There will be a day when they make you smile and not cry. Love you too!

Jonathan

I recommend writing letters to your deceased one and then you should put the letter away and answer it a day or two later. It's very cathartic and you would be surprised the answers you get! I think I read about this in a book about grief and I thought it was useless, as if any exercise could take away the pain, but it did help. I know that while you are deep in pain, the effort to write letters may be too hard, but try. It changed the endless questions I had looping through my brain. I was eventually able to add into the loop, "let it go," which Jonathan recommended in his letter to me that I wrote. "I miss you. I miss you. Why? Why wasn't I there? I love you." and Jonathan replied, "Mom, you just have to let it go." And after awhile I was even able to add another mantra into my loop of thoughts, "I still have a daughter."

We started to go to church again. We thought that would help us find some answers or maybe give us some peace or make us happier. The depression was crushing. I didn't know what to do. The minister at Jonathan's funeral was amazing so we basically went to hear him speak. Whatever your faith is I don't know how you couldn't be inspired by him. Oddly, the topic he was working on was "thrive". That sounded great to me. I wanted to turn survive into thrive, but first I needed to survive.

I grew up in the same Methodist Church. We went regularly and were involved. As a small child I didn't question whether there was a God. It seemed that no one did. Of course there is a God. As I got older, the scientific side of my brain wanted actual proof. I just had a very hard time with the faith part. How do you make yourself have faith? And right when I started questioning myself, we started to have a lot of issues in my family. My Dad started not coming home and not paying bills. We went from a normal suburban family with a working Dad and stay at home Mom to an abandoned family fearful in every moment we would be homeless. During this time I prayed every night for my Dad to come home, for the bills to be paid, for food, all of the above. He never came home, or I should say rarely. My hope turned to anger and then death, death to God. He doesn't exist. I was one of those people offended by the cross. I mocked people who believed in fairytales. For ten solid years I had only faith in myself.

By this time I was about 25 and living on my own in Chicago going to podiatry school. I hadn't had any parental or spiritual guidance in a long time and I hadn't been making the best decisions. I was constantly in a pickle, you might say. I had two friends that were very religious and although I respected them having their own opinions I did not take any of their religious advice. They would tell me I needed to pray. Yes. What good does that do? My Dad never came home…I even was dragged to a school religious group. They said it would change my life. Well it didn't. I didn't even know what they were talking about, but the free pizza was good!

One day, I really felt like my life was spiraling out of control. Why me? I'm a good person I thought to myself. Why do all these bad things keep happening? Honestly my problems weren't that bad, but they weren't that good either. I had a hard time concentrating because I was always worried about my mom and her dealing with the divorce, worried about a boyfriend cheating on me, or a guy stalking me. My grades were very up and down depending on how well I could block out the static in my head. And honestly I drank a lot. I liked to go out and have fun and push those worries aside! And when I drank? Good lord, who knows what could happen. I might give a guy a foot massage in a bar. I might go up to the stage and recite an impromptu poem. I might wear a wig and dance on top of the bar. I had so much fun, but then I had to deal with all my consequences. So, I was sitting there not knowing the first step to get my life in order when I just decided why not? Why not pray? I asked God to give me a sign. I never say what the sign is because it's kind of embarrassing, but let's just say it never happened before. I had no reason to think it ever would happen. So, when it did happen 30 minutes later, I knew it was a sign! I had said, if I got my sign, I would try to be open to God.

I am a person that sticks to promises so I did open the door. Instead of saying I was an atheist, I said I was open to the possibility. I didn't really know how to just start believing in God. I didn't even really know what that meant.

About a month later I was on a bus in Chicago and a man in a dark suit came up to me and just said, "God is waiting for you. He will always be there for you no matter how long it takes. He never leaves you even when you don't believe." I was stunned. That had a huge impact on me and really started me on my religious journey as an adult. It wasn't easy and it wasn't like I was "born again", but instead of ignoring all the questions that had turned me away from religion in the first place I tried to find answers. That takes awhile! About the time Jonathan died I was at the point where I did believe in God, but I didn't know God and to be honest I wasn't always following God's words.

Because we liked our minister so much, it did spur us on to go to church and for myself it was very helpful. I remember one topic was why to bad things happen to good people? Why is there disease and war? People say that things happen for a reason. What could be the reason for my son's death? I just wish I could explain how he was the least possible person you think would think would end his life. I wish I could explain how perfectly boring our lives were. There was no drama, no drugs, no abuse, no fighting. We got up for work and got the kids to school and went to their activities, went on family vacations, have an amazing extended family. I worked 110% to be a good mom. I looked at my kids as individuals and tried to honor their differences and tried to teach them that that is how they were special. I tried to help them see their differences as gifts and how they could use them to their advantage. I even considered letting my son take flying lessons at about age ten because I actually thought it would be a good thing. I wish I would have. So there were many topics that were relevant in our minds that the minister discussed and gave us scripture to read on the issues and that at least gave us some tools to work with.

We had cards and cards coming in, hundreds. We had meals coming every day for about five months. We had flowers delivered. CDs dropped off. Jessica's school scheduled several get togethers so she would never be alone. My community was very, very good to us. People always ask, "What should I do?". Don't ask that question! Just do something. We have no idea what is going to help us. My advice is do anything. It all helped me. But if you want to know what helped me out the most, here is my list. Someone gave me a special blend of relaxing tea which really was soothing. The books on grief were amazing and several on the afterlife. One of my favorite books was Glad No Matter What, by Sark. Another person had a candle made with Jonathan's picture on it and I cherished that. Someone gave me a copy of a birthday card Jonathan had given her daughter years past. Someone gave me a soft blanket That was a nice touch to have while I watched my endless movies. A gift certificate for massage did help me breath. Don't feel like you need to be a best friend to stop by or take a person out for coffee. If your grieving friend is not up to it, she will tell you. I can't tell you how much it all helped. It was very comforting to see who dropped off the meal and usually it came with a warm message. It really did make us feel like people cared. Even the smallest things like a hug or whisper in my ear, "I'm so sorry," helped me get through the day. Please never doubt yourself. There are no rules when it comes to supporting grieving people. We received cards from strangers that were beautiful and so thoughtful.

I am sharing one card, that was sent to us by an anonymous student from his middle school, which was very soothing. "I never knew Jonathan. But I can tell how people are reacting that he must have been an awesome person, peer and friend. A loss works in weird ways, first comes pain, then confusion, then understanding. Sometimes I wish the understanding would come first so the pain and confusion would be easier to handle. When I lost my great grandmother I was in much sorrow. But then I cherished the moments I had with her. I kept her jewelry locked up in a box and whenever I feel alone, I open it and smell. Her scent is still there and even though my memory grows fuzzy, every now and then by thinking, by remembering, she always will be with me. Ever since 2010. I have some advice, always keep Jonathan in your heart. I remember feeling like I never got to say goodbye but over the years I realized I did. It's hard to let go, to say goodbye, you may think that when you say goodbye you are forgetting him, but deep down inside Jonathan will always be inside the hearts of all that mourn him." This is so wise and so very very touching. It really did give me hope. Thank you so much whoever did send us this note.

I'm writing this in part to help people. So. they can learn what grief is like, how to help people going through it or themselves. I used religion, God winks (the signs), friends taking me out, travel. All good things. They all helped. But don't kid yourself. It's two years later and the same laundry basket with the same clothes in it the day he died are still in my closet. Boxes and boxes from our move still unpacked. His belongings remain unsorted. I still have not ordered his headstone for his grave. It hurts too much. Some of these things I will have to deal with, like the headstone. Maybe I'll be able to listen to my favorite song again. Most likely I will just donate the boxes of clothes and throw away the dirty ones. Still two years later, I'm able to get through my responsibilities and make it through the day, but once I don't have those things to keep me occupied I still fall apart and stay in bed.

So the funeral was over, the cards sent and read, the phone calls were made, the thank you cards written. If I thought I was in bad shape before, things only got worse. Endless seconds without my son. Torture. Imagine drops of water pounding on your forehead that start as drips and eventually bruise and then wound the skin and after sometime, the drip starts to feel like a hammer and your mind just has to go somewhere else to avoid the pain. Instead of drops of water though, they are endless memories of Jonathan. I understand why people "cut". My choice of physical pain was to pinch myself really hard. I did that also to remind myself that yes, I was alive and in this world. Having a physical outlet for what I was feeling inside would at least keep the wolves at bay.

My brain was a void. Conversations forgotten. Bills left unpaid. I went through so many red lights it's frightening! Once I took a left turn on a red light and headed straight into an oncoming car. He screeched his brakes. We looked into each others eyes. I didn't even care. Was it God or Jonathan that saved me? It felt like it. I thought it was Jonathan's way of showing me that God can save you if you are meant to live. I was very calm about being an inch from death. I thought to myself, well I almost joined you Jonathan just as casual as could be. I had a patient that kept needing a receipt. She kept reminding me and I would say I would send it. She had no idea the shape I was in at the end of the day and even if I did remember, the task of finding an envelope was beyond me. One day she screamed at me, "How hard is it to mail a receipt!". I knew I had to back away from my patient load. Mailing a receipt was akin to walking on water. Impossible.

One thing I hated to do was to shop for groceries. First there was the issue of getting the energy to get in the car to drive there and then there was the issue of the actual shopping. I had a system in the store. Start in the fruit section and grab Honey Crisp apples for Jonathan. Stop in shock and realize he's dead. Oh my God, feel the shock and stabbing pain all over while your body is frozen reaching for the apples as you try to compose yourself. Next I notice someone I think I might have met years ago is staring at me and wondering whether she should come over. She looks away and doesn't. I get on with my shopping and then I see someone I know and they start to cry and then I start to cry. You hug each other and I feel a bit of comfort, ok I can do this. I turn the corner into the canned fruit section and come face to face with children that went to school with Jonathan. Their eyes stare in sorrow and follow me down the aisle, but neither of us know what to say. Then in my peripheral vision I see someone I know. I'm deciding whether to acknowledge her and I look up to see that she is steadfastly looking away and then abruptly turns into the next aisle. Ok, that was helpful, thanks! I've finished only about a third of my shopping, but I have to leave immediately before I burst into sobs. I make it to the car as the tears start to roll and let it rip inside the car. Why is this happening to me? Why me? IT'S NOT FAIR.

So, I know this is a really uncomfortable topic and no one knows what to do, but I have to talk about. When Jonathan died, it was like a bomb dropped in our community. Everyone knew about it. Everyone was shocked. Everyone was grieving. I felt like I was under a microscope. I felt like everywhere I went people were staring and me and for the most part that was true. I remember meeting someone for the first time and after I said my name, she got a startled look on her face and clammed up, not knowing whether to say something to me or not and then I didn't know what to do. I ran into a friend I hadn't seen in years and she nervously was telling me about a flying squirrel in her bedroom as to avoid the most obvious topic. I have no hard feelings towards this person. I know it's so awkward. I only tell the squirrel story so that people can learn from my experience. Saying nothing is almost worse than saying the wrong thing. It just made me feel horrible. I found that just being straight forward and honest was the best policy. A stranger came up to me in the parking lot of Target, a mom obviously, and she just lightly touched my arm and said, "I am so sorry. You don't know me, but

I just want you to know that everyone is thinking about you and we are here for you." I just thanked her and she went on her way. Another mom just openly said she didn't know what to say. That's fine too. I just hated those shifty moments where I was talking to someone and they just couldn't look me in the eye. I get it. It was hard for them too. If at all possible though, try to just act normal around me. I was comfortable around my friends. They let me lead and were just there. It was the social events like the swim banquet or even just getting gas that were so uncomfortable and just made me want to crawl back in my dark hole. You should assume a grieving person is doing pretty awful, but no one wants to admit that. I had someone just come out and say, "This just sucks. Death sucks." That made me laugh! So true! If you want to know what always makes people happy is telling them memories about their loved ones! And my last thing on this topic is even if it's been a year and this is the first time you are seeing me, it needs to be addressed otherwise it's just a weird thing. It's never too late to offer a shoulder to cry on or give a hug to ease the pain. Don't make the grieving person do the hard work and expect them to say something. They have enough on their plate. All you really need to say is "I'm sorry.".

I was really gracious and understanding towards all the comments that made me feel weird. I feel like we can do better though. I put myself in that same group because I once said the same ridiculous things like, "stay strong" to a grieving person, as if they weren't the strongest person alive to even get out of bed in the morning. I too assumed that my friend who lost her Dad would be fine two months later because she knew her Dad was sick and she had a whole year to say goodbye. I didn't know that the missing feeling was sheer misery and it never really goes away completely. I didn't know how transforming grief is. I do now. That's why I'm writing about it so we can start talking about grief not because I just want to point out proper grief etiquette. I do hope that this is helpful information.

We tried to keep my daughter as busy as possible. Suddenly losing a sibling and being an only child was traumatic and she couldn't bear to be alone. She was afraid in the house and wouldn't even be there alone for a second. One time she got home from school a few minutes early and I was coming home from work and I found her waiting outside in winter weather. Better to freeze than to deal with sitting alone on the couch where they used to do their homework and watch TV. People their whole lives thought they were twins. They were only 18 months apart and my son was tall for his age. They used to argue all day and night. "JONATHAN!!!!" was a frequent scream I heard and of course, "MOM she kicked me!". The house was silent as an empty church. And that hurt. It still does. That was my daughter's way of dealing with things. Be crazy. Get together with friends. Listen to music. Have fun. Shut out the sadness. Squeeze yourself so it doesn't hurt. It did get her through the day, but I knew the day would come when the dam would crack and the emotions would overtake her. I was afraid it would happen in college where she wouldn't have any support. I really wanted her to start therapy. She was adamant. She wasn't talking to the therapist!

My husband, on the other hand was an open raw sore and if I touched that sore, boy I got the roar of a big black bear! We were his whipping post for his 50 lashes, emotionally speaking, especially me. It's hard to fight when you are not grieving even harder when you are and of course I would lash back. It was an awful time and I feel so bad that my daughter had to live through this. We were supposed to be taking care of her. She lost her brother and she was losing her parents. I remember one night Jon called and said he was going to this restaurant for carry out and did I want anything. I said, "Yes, I'll have my salad." I ordered the same salad from the same place for 15 years and we joked about it. It was "my salad". So he said, "What salad?". I thought he was joking, but I said, "You know. The one I always get…". He said, "Just give me a name." I didn't remember the name but I thought it was the Alexander salad maybe? So when he got home and I saw it was the wrong salad and commented on that you'd think I'd have just slapped his Mom. This sent him on a rage that just had my daughter and I speechless. I left the house. I was going to stay in a hotel. I sat in the parking lot of the Kingsley Inn and just could not believe this was happening. I was going to stay in a hotel? But then again, could I go home to that? I'm telling you, this is not who we were. We were laid back and fun loving! Ultimately I didn't want to waste the money so I went home. We acknowledged it was just the sadness and so we calmed down, but nothing was fixed.

Jonathan, you went first and showed me that I don't have to be afraid. I will look forward to all of Jessica's milestones and know you will be with us. You may even know my unborn children now. I know you have two siblings up there and Dylan's older brother. Have you met them yet? I know it can take a long time to be connected with them. I know you have tried so hard to help us down here on earth, but keep trying. Don't give up on Daddy! Love you bud! Goodnight!.

Through the pain I had glimmers of insight that helped. What you may not know is even one positive thought in the day could illuminate a space and that gave me hope even if it was for just a moment.

I had a dream we were at a swim meet and you were laying on a towel on the deck. I called to you and you opened your eyes and I was so happy! He is alive! I asked if you were ok and you said, "Yeah I think so." Then I looked at your teeth and saw they were broken and said that I thought we should still go to the ER. You contemplated that and agreed with me. I was looking around to find someone and tell them we were going to the ER and we were walking together when suddenly you walked towards a door and said you would be waiting outside and you walked out. Then I realized that this cannot be fixed. We are not going to the ER .I woke up. Sorry so sorry this can't be fixed!

The holidays were upon us. Jonathan died on November 13, just a few weeks before Thanksgiving. What I remember most vividly is being so thankful to have a few days off because working had been unbearable. People had commented in awe that I had gone back to work thinking mistakenly that is was a good sign. I was just following my orders. I had been given the message to get up and get going so I did but it took such effort! It's moments like this I wish I was a writer so I could adequately explain the exhaustion. Even sleep was work. I almost dreaded it. It gave no relief nor did it replenish my energy. My family had planned to run the 5K Turkey Trot in downtown Detroit, but that was out of the question for me. I needed that vacation for pure rest. My two sisters and one of their sons did go and ran it in honor of Jonathan. I guess it was a point to say, yes, we can, in spite of it all.

The run started with the Star Spangled Banner, a gift for my family knowing how much Jonathan loved that song and it was a good way to start the run. My nephew, Sean, had eaten a chocolate muffin before the run and was getting cramps from it. Usually he would be up front, urging his mom on, but this time he was struggling. They walked. They ran. They walked. Towards the end Sean was feeling like he wouldn't make it, when the song It's My Life, by Bon Jovi came on. Another song from Jonathan! Sean says that it felt like his feet were lifted each step he took and suddenly he had a burst of energy that propelled him to the finish line! Jonathan is with us. You hear of people saying they feel a hand on their shoulder and turn around and no one is there, well Sean said he felt something actually pushing him from behind. Miraculous. So, on this Thanksgiving, I was thankful for that sign. I have to keep reminding myself that he IS still with us.

We made it through Thanksgiving, but still loomed ahead. I always made a big deal about Christmas. The tree went up the day after Thanksgiving. We made gingerbread houses. We did the shelf elf. We went to Meadowbrook Hall, an American castle owned by the late Matilda Dodge Wilson, to see it decorated. We went to the Christmas dinner at our club. We watched the Polar Express 20 times. We went sledding and drank hot chocolate after. The list goes on. I wasn't a perfectionist, I just love Christmas. The first Christmas was just sadness, no joy. I look at pictures of us during that time but I just see blank stares. I did force myself to do a few things. I remember crying while I was shopping as I passed the boys section. There was such a big hole in my life. You could say my body was a hole and I as a physical entity did not exist. It's hard to explain, but there were times that I was not conscious of having a body. I just felt pure pain that went beyond the confines of my body. The few things we did, all we could think about was how happy Jonathan would have been if he was here. What funny things he would have done. For example he always took all the candy canes that were laid out for decoration at our club and stuffed them in his pockets. We did that for him that year!

One Sunday that December we were at church and I don't remember the exact topic, but our minister said something like, "We are all God's children and everything he does, he does for us. Imagine that your child wants to do something and you have to tell him no. The child will just get mad and not understand, but you know you are doing what's best in the long run. They may or may not ever know that decisions you make for them lead to good things. God is our parent and he is always helping us even when we think he is not." That was a very good message for me. I spent all day dwelling on this. It is an incredible leap of faith to think that losing my son could lead to good things. I didn't think I could quite accept that yet.

We also had an opportunity to be re baptized. It was a simple procedure, but symbolic. I really needed any support I could get. I do feel that God was helping me, holding up my body. It was like a supernatural force was keeping us from just folding into thin air. That night I had the most extraordinary experience.

I had a dream that I was driving around all day seeing patients and getting stressed because I HAD to get to the DMV. I kept having all these delays like construction, and an accident blocking the road, patients that had extra problems and I was so frustrated! I was elated as I pulled into the parking lot 10 minutes before close time. I went in and stood in line. The woman at the desk was a jolly woman about 55 with blonde curly hair and she chatted with each customer as they went through the line. When I got to the front, I handed her my papers and she looked at them and told me, "Sorry. You're too late. You missed the deadline. No license for you." I was so confused as to why I couldn't get a license. There is no deadline for that. It's not a good idea to let your license lapse, but you could always renew it. No, she was adamant. I explained to her how much I needed to drive. My job is driving around seeing home bound patients. She was getting annoyed with me and I asked to talk to a manager. Then she looked at me and screamed, "YOU NEED TO TAKE A BREAK FROM THIS JOB!". I woke up out of the dream and was just completely startled. What am I supposed to do? Am I supposed to quit my job? Take a vacation? Focus on my family more? What did she mean? Who was that woman?

As I was thinking about this, a very strange thing happened. Ok so normally when you close your eyes you just see darkness and maybe a few flickers of color or a haze of light. I was seeing the inside of my brain. It was like a picture- perfect image of my brain, but I wasn't just seeing what the brain looked like I was seeing how it worked. All the messages flying back and forth to various parts of the brain. And I was simultaneously seeing things happen in the brain. In this area popcorn was being popped. In this area a bicycle wheel was spinning and more. I was astounded. I really did not understand how this was happening. And it was so fast and complex I had a hard time following it in order to figure out what was going on. Suddenly in the middle of my brain, a flower started to bloom. The petals started to uncurl and expand, the roots started to grow into my brain. I could feel the physical pressure of something pushing on my brain. It was uncomfortable, not quite painful so I yelled at my brain to "STOP!" and it did.

I was completely freaked out at this point. You don't understand. Nobody would understand. I was looking at the inside of my brain. I was awake. This was not a dream. This was not an imaginary thought. Where did it come from? How did this happen? What happened next is almost impossible to describe. I will try to, but there are no words adequate. It was not a dream!

As I lay there thinking about the crazy dream and then awakening to a tour of my brain, I was trying to figure out the connection. I then became aware of an orange orb glowing a few feet in front of me. It was small, maybe a foot in diameter. It came closer to me and then floated to the middle of the room where it changed to a blueish color and expanded to about 5 feet. The weirdest thing is that when my eyes were open it was like it was just a light in my room. I could see everything in my room just like it was normal, but in addition a glowing light. If I closed my eyes it was like it was me in a dark space, just me and and the orb. But it wasn't just that I was seeing this in my mind or seeing this in my room. Imagine that when you close your eyes, your body is not who you are and what you see is not with your eyes, but with your mind. When I closed my eyes it was if it was a vast universe in front of me and I was seeing some alternative place. If I opened my eyes I still saw the light but it was in the context of my room.

So the orb of light started to spin and it went so fast it turned into a white light and then it exploded into a thousand stars or just bits of electricity and then there would be a sort of blob of a figure that would slowly define itself into an angel. The wings were always defined, but the body was somewhat lucid and only some- what of shape similar to a person. This process would take maybe 5 minutes and I would only see the angel just long enough to say to myself yes, this in an angel. Then I started to see ribbons of colors, mostly purple, pink, and blue and they mixed with each other and then disappeared into a smoke like fog and then reappeared and melted like a lava lamp. It was very entertaining actually, so I just watched it and then another orb came in and got bigger and brighter and did the same thing. It spun into an angel again. This went on for at least an hour and a half or so. I even got up to get something to drink and sit in wonder by the Christmas tree and still it continued.

After some time passed, I started to see visions of things. It was like seeing a movie all around you in a 3D Imax. First I was seeing an ancient village which reminded me of Turkey or Aladdin. It was gold, beige, and magenta, and very, very old. I was taken down alleys around corners, through houses and flew above the city. Then that was over and I was skiing down a mountain and snow was flying at me and I was seeing avalanches.

My attention would be drawn to a branch covered in snow and I just thought, why is that branch important? And I could feel the snow coming at me and hitting my face. Next was flashes of different buildings, just structural parts, as if the blueprints were the building, and I was seeing the mechanics of an elevator, a clock, and more. I just kept wondering why am I seeing this? That was probably another hour.

Then suddenly I was being pulled through a tunnel of stars. I could feel my head being pulled and just surrounded by stars. After a time I was at the end of the tunnel and I came out into a forest. Around me were trees and sunsets of all different colors and they kept changing. Sometimes I would be on the ground looking up and sometimes I would be above looking down. It was spectacular. Sunsets are one of my favorite things. They always perk me up and I always pointed them out to my kids, so many times making them run outside to see the sky. At this point, I just enjoyed watching the sunsets. I didn't think about why or how this was happening. I was just relaxed and accepting. And then just as sudden as could be there was Jonathan's face filling the space and looking at me with his blue blue eyes and then boom, an American flag flapping through in the air. It was a shock to the body, a blow. My heart skipped a beat. I knew it was him, his energy and that made me happy, but I also wanted to touch him, to reach in there and hold him, but that didn't happen.

After that I was dumbfounded. I didn't even have the energy to think about what had just happened. I was surrounded by the colors again and I slowly drifted off to sleep.

I woke up and instead of having that dreadful realization that Jonathan was dead, I had a sense of wonder. I didn't have any doubts that it happened. However I didn't know how to process it. I wanted to know HOW it happened. In my gut I do believe I was given a vision of Jonathan's heaven and he showed me that he is ok and we will have connections throughout my life. I can still connect with my son. What a gift! This doesn't happen to many people! I am giving you, my readers, this gift. Your loved one is still with you. I know this without a shadow of doubt. You can connect with them also! Your connection with them is eternal. This was possibly one of the most impactful experiences in my life second to child birth. I know people might think that I had a psychotic episode, but it didn't feel like one. I was aware of my actual surroundings and I was questioning what was happening. I had the opportunity to see beyond the veil of what we consider reality and the surprising thing is, it is right here in front of us. In fact we live among it. Yet for most of us, and most of the time we don't see it. But now I know that so much more is possible in this world. It is far from black and white, it is even more than a rainbow, it is infinity possibilities. There is so much more possible in this world that we could even imagine and it is all connected to love.

I read a lot of books and spent time googling articles to find answers to my questions. I mainly wondered how did this happen to me? Two books that I read, the writers had similar experiences or similar enough for me to relate to them, are The Afterlife of Billy Fingers, by Annie Kagan and The Hand on the Mirror, by Janis Heaphy Durham. The writers seem like logical, practical people (not psychics or mediums) that had extremely unique and unbelievable things happen to them. I was so relieved to know others had gone through this and were sane enough to write books about them later. In fact that is why I am writing this now!

In Billy Fingers, Annie is contacted by her dead brother and she is told her job is to write down Billy's experiences in the afterlife. Her book is a description of what happens after a person dies. A very interesting read and it confirmed what I saw in my "vision". Annie hears her dead brother talking to her and she recites his story for him. He describes being in a chamber of silvery blue lights and goes through a tunnel "floating blissfully through stars". He is no longer a body, but he feels like he has one and it is being healed. So he was describing something similar to what I had seen. I don't think it was a coincidence that I read this book. I felt like so many of the books correlated with things that happened or what I was feeling at the moment. It was consoling to think Jonathan was healing in the afterlife. Now I believe that I did learn that also from my minister, but I always need more proof. My scientific mind was still resisting a bit, wondering if I was crazy, but my vision was so beautiful and touching why wouldn't I want to believe it?

In the book, The Hand in the Mirror, the author experiences things that confirm that life does not end with our physical death. She wakes on the one year anniversary of her husband's death to find his hand print on her mirror. She also had things in her home move. Nobody else was in her home. The author researches and meets with many scientists that study the afterlife and goes to retreats to learn more about contacting spirits and how this is done. Without retelling her story, this satisfied the scientific side of my mind. I needed to know that a scientific type person experienced this and collaborated with others to prove physically that this happened. She didn't just experience this in her mind. She had physical proof. Maybe one day I will also have the opportunity to travel to these facilities and have my experiences validated by others, but in the meantime, I will rely on Janis Durham's information in her book.

This was a huge step in my healing process. Knowing that somewhere Jonathan was existing, healing, growing, and at the same time he was with me. This was substantial. A small weight was lifted. Still, missing him was agonizing. I don't wake up and relive his death anymore, but there was still an intense hole in me that I felt the instant I woke up. I just miss him. I can hear him laugh at me like, "Seriously, Mom? I gave you visions. You know I'm ok. Why are you still sad?". I agree. I'm so thankful to know he is ok. I don't just think he is ok, I know he is. I just miss that I won't be able to see him graduate. I won't see him get married. I won't see him grow up.

"Remember, Jonathan, when you used to see patients with me? Remember the patient that gave you the raccoon? Remember the Russian patient that told you Jonathan sounded like apple in Russian. You were a good little helper sitting next to me and examining everything I did as I worked with my patients. And you are handsome and beautiful and kind and funny and different. And I love you for it!".

"Jonathan, my mind goes in every direction trying to figure this out. I know that somewhere you are ok, but still, WHY? A mother's love is not enough I guess. Daddy is lost without you. Broken. You were his best friend. I know that this is bigger than that though. That we must learn our life lessons here on earth. Still just seems TOO much. TOO unbelievable. TOO cruel. You were so funny! Will we ever laugh like that again?".

That night started a series of visions, dreams, and signs that regularly occurred for several months. Anytime I closed my eyes I saw a big purple circle in my mind. If I sat for awhile the circle would melt and start changing shape and then turn blue and I would just watch the colors float around my mind. This was soothing, I considered that purple circle to be like a friend. As long as the circle was with me, I would feel ok, kind of like a security blanket. Some times, the colors would coalesce into Jonathan's face, one time it was a hand waving at me. It was helpful in getting to sleep, kind of mesmerizing. I know this is all so strange, but it did happen.

So we got through Thanksgiving and Christmas loomed ahead. We went to Meadowbrook Hall, an "American castle" previously owned by Matilda Dodge Wilson of the Dodge automobile company. It is open to the public for tours and is decorated lavishly for Christmas. We had gone several years to see this. The kids got a kick out of the secret passageways that were in the house and between the kids playrooms. The last year I had taken the kids' Christmas card photo there and they had brutally argued with each other and me because they did not want to take the photo. I admonished them both, telling them that memories are important. Someday they would cherish this photo. That memory was heavy on my mind that day. We were sad to be there without him, but also proud of ourselves for making it off the couch and getting outside. Early on we had a feeling of us against the world. Only we could understand each other. We were solidified by our sadness.

As I earlier stated, this was my favorite holiday. We used to watch the Polar Express over and over and I would be so happy to see my kids get excited for the big day. This time, we watched with tears. I used to hide the shelf elf and my kids would try to wake up first to find it and they rushed around frantically to be the one to find it. This year, he remained hidden for several days in a row, the fun of finding him was gone without Jonathan competing with Jessica. She would eventually find it, but half the fun of finding the prize with the elf was to lord it over her brother. It just wasn't the same without him. We had always gone to the Christmas dinner at our club and it felt absolutely wrong without him, but at the same time we didn't want to ruin Jessica's Christmas so we went. I remembered all the things he used to do. One year he wore an elf hat and helped at the coat check. One year he took home a Nutcracker decoration in his pocket. One year he ran up to Santa and almost pulled off his beard. We didn't actually have fun that night. I guess we just had to prove to ourselves that we could go.

The shopping was very sad. My daughter was showered that Christmas with gifts and I would have done anything to make her happy. Later, we would learn that material objects are not too helpful with grief. I watched movies all day. Breakfast at Tiffany's was one that distracted me and gave me moments of relief. I would recommend comedies and feel good movies while grieving. That definitely helped me!

We had my family and a few friends over for Christmas Eve dinner. That night the cousins and friends wrote memories on red and green construction paper strips and then we stapled them together and made a chain of memories. Remember when Jonathan pretended to be a raccoon for a week and would only talk to you if you talked in raccoon speak? Remember when he went deep sea fishing and the seals jumped in his boat? Remember when he went snorkeling without his suit in the British Virgin Islands because he was too sunburned to wear it? It helped them feel like he was still there. Jonathan's antics were epic. We had a lot to talk about! We strung the chain around the doorway of his room and there they stayed until we moved. Everyone is different, but talking about Jonathan always fills the hole a bit for me. I have to acknowledge him. I don't want people to forget him.

Jon and I used to stay up until one am or so wrapping presents in our back bathroom, after the kids were well asleep in a food coma from their customary candy cane milkshake. We put the presents under the tree and stood back and held hands and proudly thought about the joy to be experienced the next morning. This time, Jon went straight to bed after dinner and the guests left and I did the wrapping by myself. I was crying while wrapping the presents and the tree looked so barren with only presents for Jessica under the tree. The last year we had given the kids skis and I remembered how much they loved them and how much Jonathan had loved to ski. I laid down after I had finished and was trying miserably to get to sleep when I had another vision. This time I saw flashes of ornaments in my mind and a scrapbook, flipping through pictures of Jessica and Jonathan at Christmas. He was sharing all his memories with me again reassuring me he was still with us. I'd like to say that helped me get through the next day, but that was a sad day. We opened our presents, gave each other hugs and retreated to our beds.

Thankfully, our friends had invited us up North for New Years. The first year, we got away as much as we could. It was very healthy for us to not be around the painful memories that were everywhere in our house and the community. I could barely drive down the street, his ghost was everywhere. I still hold my breath when I pass his school. For awhile I fought an urge to throw bricks through the school windows. We don't know what happened, but I believe those walls in the school do. It was good to be away from all that and friends usually could keep my mind off the misery for short periods of time, but if I needed I could be open with my feelings of loss and have their support.

Our friends had given us gift certificates for massages. For you grieving people, if you can afford it, massage was very helpful for me. My shoulders were always hunched up and stiff from stress, so not only was it relaxing, but it allowed me to open up and breath better. Initially for me, massage therapy was more helpful than tradition therapy with a counselor. I didn't want to talk and I didn't want to relive his death.

We drank a lot of champagne, played Cards Against Humanity, had the fireplace going continuously and took walks out in the snow filled city. One day as I was walking it began to snow, a white out and it was blowing straight into my face and it was exactly like in my first vision and then I looked to my right and there was a snow covered branch exactly like I had seen also. I had wondered why I was being shown a branch and now I knew that it was telling me that Jonathan would be with me at that moment. That was a surprise and it made me smile.

That night we put messages for Jonathan on lanterns and lifted them into the sky. We watched them go up, up, and far away, all the way to heaven. These symbolic gestures were always a great help to me. It made me feel like I was doing something. It also was a way for me to feel and show Jonathan that we still loved him.

On the morning of the first of the year, my friend and I went to a meditation class. We sat in silence in the warmth of the room. Thoughts went in and out of my mind, but I was able to feel some peace. My thoughts were not jagged and painful at this moment, as they normally were. The trip had eased the pain a bit. I just felt sad. As I was sitting on my cushion I started to see the colors stream through my mind. For ten minutes I was enjoying my light show of colors and then pure black. All of a sudden there was a spotlight in my mind and then confetti burst into the blackness. "Happy New Year Mom!" Spectacular!

I was seeing visions all the time in my mind. I have no idea what most of them mean. Sometimes I couldn't even tell what I was seeing. Some of the odder visions I had were molten gold, bubbling and brewing, lots of buildings, and once I saw a white robe flowing in the wind and bare feet. I have read a lot to try and understand what I was seeing and why. I feel like most of the time these were symbols that spirits were using to give me messages. The only message I was interested in though was to know where Jonathan was and to know he is ok. I can only assume that if spirits exist that can give me messages, most likely Jonathan is one too. These are huge leaps of faith, and had I not experienced this almost everyday, I wouldn't have believed it. I started asking everyone when I found a loved one had passed if they sent them messages. So many people said yes. Many people told me stories about seeing angels, Jesus, vivid visits in dreams. It seems I was not the only one. People just don't talk about it.

I had a patient that told me a story about her daughter. They were in the hospital. The doctor had told her that her daughter would not make it through the night. This was before antibiotics and her daughter had a serious infection. My patient was not going to leave her daughter for one second. She had been holding her hand praying for a miracle as her daughter lay there like a rag doll. Suddenly her daughter sat up a bit and looked at the foot of the bed and smiled. She told her mom it would be ok. She was going to be fine. Her mother asked her how did she know? The little girl said Jesus told her. He was there at the foot of her bed healing her. Her mom, startled and thinking perhaps she was in delirium, asked her what did Jesus look like and her daughter said, "the most beautiful person in the world". Her daughter did survive and went on to lead a very healthy life.

I work with mostly elderly patients who have experienced multiple losses so I was told many many stories like this. Most of these people didn't even know that I had lost a son. I think I only told a handful of patients. I could not have worked for one second if they asked about my son. I was always one eyelash away from breaking down in tears for almost a year. So unbeknownst to my patients, they thought they were unburdening themselves with their stories, but they were healing me.

I had another patient in her 90s and she had dementia. She said almost the same thing every time I saw her, "Am I your last patient? I hope you get to go home soon. You are the nicest person. Am I your last patient?". I answered all her questions over and over as if I had never been asked. Each visit it was the same questions. One visit about 2 to 3 months after Jonathan died she looked at me and said, "I've had the MOST amazing life. I've traveled around the world. I won gardening awards. I've done everything I ever wanted. I have a beautiful family." "Oh how many kids do you have," I asked? "Well, I had 3, but one died in a car accident. He had a brand new red Mustang convertible and he drove it as fast as he could. That was really sad, but you can get over it and then you will have the most amazing life." It was so strange how so many people had hidden messages for me. They didn't even know it! And honestly I couldn't ever imagine ever making it more than a few more years. The thought that I could live till I was 90 and say my life was amazing was a miraculous thought, but here this woman did it, so MAYBE I could too.

Dear Jonathan,

You were a challenge from the day you came home. Refusing, absolutely refusing to use the bassinet we bought JUST FOR YOU. We would have to hold you for a long time and then rock you in your car seat. You wanted to be held all the time. You cried uncontrollably with the sitter at the gym. That was the reason I stopped working out! You argued with me at every turn. But I loved every minute. I considered these to be your talents. It may have made my life harder, but I knew that although you appeared to be argumentative and stubborn, you were really a lover, deeply passionate, and a just person and that eventually these traits that drove a mother crazy would create a successful person. I knew you would stand up for yourself. I knew you would be handsome, smart young man. I wish I would have told you that more often.

Love, Mom

Dear Mom,

You are right I was confident in my opinions and I did believe in justice. I was also extremely sensitive. Things that didn't bother other people, I took to heart. Sometimes the world just seemed too cruel to me. You thought I just had problems that any normal 12 year old had and that's true. They just didn't seem normal to me. I regret that I didn't share my fears with you, but I wanted you to be proud of me and not think I was weak. I'm with you always mom. You can still tell me whatever is in your heart anytime.

Love,
Jonathan

Two months had passed. Every morning I still woke up and realized all over again that you were gone. My heart broke everyday. The only way out, I thought was to be a better person and serve God. I felt like the lesson I needed to learn was to take full advantage of my physical life and the ability to taste, smell and feel. To live large. But I was still and am still confused on how to do this? Is it photography? Is it reflexology? Is it family? My present to you is to transform myself so that your death will not be in vain.

"I love you buddy. I used to see such depth in your eyes. You looked at me with trust and I can still remember the night before when we talked about your detention and how you looked at me. I felt like we understood each other. I know you felt misunderstood by a lot of people, but we had a special bond. You might have had Dad's body, but you had my quirks. You were hurt by some also. But I didn't think it would come to this.

Right now I am just putting my trust in God. That it was your time. That I could not change this. That you are taken care of. That I will see you again.

I imagined that the sun that was so big in the sky was a gift from you. I feel like you are in the snow and the wind and the trees and saying hello to me.

So here I am, one day at a time.

One moment I am ok enough to have positive thoughts like that, only the very next second to be dragged down in a crushing wave and be smashed against the bottom of the ocean across broken sharp shells, salty water entering my nose and choking me.

Oh dear. I cannot believe it still. I remember feeling for the pulse and there wasn't one. I can still see your crystal clear blue eyes staring at me. I can still see your braces and being angry we would never see what your beautiful smile would look like. This is not my life. This is not happening to me. One step at a time, one horrible step."

My sister, Paula, set me up with a medium that had been referred to her. When she called to set it up, the medium was just given my first name. The medium asked my sister, had she lost a dad? My sister said no, and the medium said well I just keep hearing, "Daddy. Daddy. Daddy." What the medium didn't know was that I wanted my husband to go, but he did not want to. So when the medium asked for our names and Paula told them Karen and Jessica, she was also wondering whether she should say Jon also, but she didn't. We think that the reading had already started and Jonathan was trying to say Daddy would be there also or he wanted Daddy to be there.

The day of the reading I cleared my head an said a prayer that I hoped Jonathan would step forward and connect with us. I hoped that we would be able to say our goodbyes, although now I know we don't have to.

So I picked up Jessica from school. I would say she was hopeful we would get a message, but a little bit skeptical. We drove to the medium's house and entered a room behind her garage. There was a new age type angel outside the door and Jessica and I exchanged a glance like, ok what are we doing?

The medium was a cheerful, normal person, she introduced herself and then we picked out a Tarot card and set them aside. Carrie, the medium, went on to explain how the reading works and how she connects to spirits. We listened, but I don't remember much of that part. I just wanted to hear from Jonathan.

When she finishes explaining the protocol, Carrie looks at me and says, "So you lost a son." "Yes", I nod. He wants us to know he is ok. Heaven is like Disneyland everyday with an unlimited credit card. She asks me, "Who is Jack?". That is my Dad, I exclaim. "Who is Eric?" I answer my brother... "Your son took things too seriously.", Carrie tells me. Yes he did I think to myself. "Who is Jon?", she again asks us? That is my husband. Then she tells me that the reading is for Jon. It is to prove to him that Jonathan does continue in the afterlife. The information we get today will verify that. She tells us to tell Jon not to feel guilty. She tells Jessica it is ok to wear the Harvard sweatshirt that was his. She can have anything she wants of his. He tells us his hair looks good now. His hair had always been trouble and I had lately been wondering what we were going to do about it. At his funeral, Jessica had commented that his hair never looked better. Now he tells us that his hair looks good all the time. "Who is Dylan?" asks Carrie. That is our good friend's son. She communicates Jonathan's many messages to us. Apparently Jonathan watches him play hockey. She tells us that Jonathan now has a pierced ear. That would not surprise me, just to stir up trouble. His Dad would never had allowed it. He is going to go to Florida with Paige when she goes down there. He wants to go to Tony's. This Jessica and I are unsure of, but ok. He wants us to have a bonfire. He says to turn his phone on. He will contact us in ways with our phones. Yes, all of us have had weird things happening with our phones. Old texts popping up and that sort of thing. He likes to play with the lights. Yes, we've noticed! We often have the lights suddenly turn off and then mysteriously turn back on hours later. Carrie asks us about the Ray Bans? Yes, they were his prized possession for Alaska. She says that he says we can have them. He wants us to plant a tree in his honor. They planted a tree at his middle school. He talks about a light house, the one in Holland. He likes to have fun. Yes, always. He says there were more people at his funeral than he thought there would be. I thought that also. He's riding a truck now. He always wanted Jon to get a truck! Carrie says he is glad I am wearing the necklace now. Yes I agree, Jonathan thank you for finding it. I always wear it now. He wants us to name a star after him. He is handsome. He's 12. He had mood swings we couldn't see. Now all the girls like him. He has a dog. Buck is with him. Buck was his Dad's dog. He was very sensitive. He is watching Seanie. His cousin. He wants us to celebrate November 13 as a birthday because that is his birthday in heaven. Dylan is his brother. Well we are very close to his family. Family best friends. His teeth are good now. Thank you. I've been bothered by his teeth this whole time. He says to stop beating ourselves up over the gun. She tells us there is something about a girl. He was in LOVE and she didn't love him back. She tells us that Patrick is praying for us. We know two neighbors named Patrick. They might be praying for us? He's worried that his Mom and Dad may grow apart. Yes, possible. It's very hard on a marriage. He wants us to go shopping at Costco. He used to beg me to join Costco, but I was boycotting it. He likes squirt guns. Oh yes, very much so. He will be in the BVI with us and send us dolphins. He tells me that I have to play more, do more. He doesn't want Christmas to suck. Yes mom, I said suck. He wondered why everyone gave me girl angels at Christmas. They should have given me boy angels. We did get multiple girl angels. I did eventually buy a boy angel. Right now he's learning about my childhood. He's living in my childhood house. I had had two dreams that he was meeting my old friends from childhood and he was in my house that I grew up in. She brings up the word "Lilac". Yes our driveway was lined with lilacs and I used to lay beneath them and look at the sky and dream. Lilac is still one of my favorite blooms and scents. She tells us he liked what we put in his casket. We put in a stuffed dog called Nippy, letters, some of his coins he collected, pictures, and a fire opal from Cabo San Lucas. She tells us he liked the lanterns we put up into the air. He asks Jessica why isn't she going to the dance? Jessica doesn't know which dance, but thinks he might mean Sadie's? He tells us it's ok to move. He says he won't haunt the house and that is something I had been worried about. Carrie tells us that he says the garage door needs to be fixed. Now that was a crazy thing for her to say! Jonathan was the garage door master and we believed he had been the one lifting it for us all these months since he died. He wants to get a root beer float. Yes he did love those! Carrie tells us that Jonathan is handing Jessica a gummy bear. He says not to spoil Jessica now that he is gone. Boy, had we been spoiling her! He tells me he wants me to do random acts of kindness. He says that will make me feel better and help me heal. She asks us, "Did someone miss a dentist's appointment?". Yes Jessica did and her rescheduled appointment was in a few days. He said he would be with her at the dentist. She tells us that Jonathan wants to know when is Dad going to make carrot cake? He says Dad is a good chef. He wants him to make macaroni and cheese. The carrot cake and Mac and cheese are two of Jonathan's favorites and everybody asks Jon to make them. He tells Jessica to save his coins. They are for her kids when she eventually has them. Jonathan likes music and is wearing his headphones. Yes I had bought him Beats and he did love those headphones! She says, "Dad hurt his knee and needs surgery but he won't have it." All true. She asks, "Who is Jen?" She's our good friend. She says Jonathan considered her a mom. Yes, he had spent a week with her family during the summer and she was like a mom to him then. She says his birthday is coming up. Yes, in a few weeks. She says he has Pancakes with him. Pancakes was Jessica's guinea pig. He wants us to know he didn't suffer. There was an angel there waiting for him. He says he likes his coffee mug. We have his coffee mug with his football picture on it displayed in the kitchen. I had gotten it a few days before he died and I asked him if he liked it and he had given me a kind of non committal comment. I always look at it and wonder if he had really liked the mug? She asks about a rubber band gun? Yes he had one! She says he says sorry, but not sorry, and is still laughing. He would always shoot Jessica with it and she would always freak out. I would tell him to stop and then he would shoot it BY her but not ON her and then look at me with a look like what did I do, Mom? She tells us to write down all the memories, the good and the bad. She tells us the cats can see him. He wants to go four wheeling with Scott. Scott is his uncle and they did used to 4 wheel together. He says Jessica doesn't need to go to a therapist, she can journal her grief. I had been trying to get Jessica to go to a therapist, but she refused to go. He tells me not to be overprotective. I am and I think I will always be. Sorry. She asks me about one shoe? One shoe is not enough? Yes. Every time I look at his one shoe in the closest, his precious custom Rochies, I wish I had the pair. The other one went in the ambulance with him and I never got it back. How I wept over that shoe. She told me he said not to worry. That at sometime I wouldn't even care about the shoe, but for now, one shoe was enough. He says Anthony has a crush on Jessica. Maybe? He says Jessica was French in another lifetime and she needs to learn the language fluently as she may have a job there someday. She does love Paris and we have talked about living there. He says she needs to learn manners. Most likely true. He delivers the information about manners with a little grin. She says he likes to leave dimes tails up and if we see one to know that it is him giving us a message. We have since found them in the strangest places! He says Jessica has been shopped out and to put the money towards a car. Yes, guilty of that again. He says, "Alexis is weird." Agree. He loves Paige. She is very gifted and can see him. She did say she saw him at his funeral. He stands by the poinsettia. That is possible and it's right by my chair. She asks "Who is Jenna?" That is his cousin. She says Jenna is having a hard time feeling everyone's sadness. Jonathan also admits to his fair share of picking on Jenna. Completely true! Thinking of the time Jonathan and his cousin Kyle locked her in the dog cage and treated her like a dog. We then got to show our Tarot cards. I picked "children" Jessica picked "truth". We were there to find out the truth of my child, indeed. He leaves us with this message, "There's only one Jonathan and there will only ever be one Jonathan. Don't name your kids after me because they will never be me." He's sorry the McKee name stops with him. He won't be here to carry it on. Lastly, Carrie tells us that he needs us to forgive him.

Jessica and I walked out of the medium's garage and looked at each other in awe. We really felt like we had been talking to Jonathan! So many details she couldn't possibly have know and there was even more that I did not share. Jessica said it was the happiest day of her life. I felt that was a true connection and although that certainly relieved me, that he was ok in heaven, I still missed him so very badly. The depression was still crushing. I shared the reading with my husband and he found it incredible. He could hardly believe she could be so spot on. Again, for all of us it was a tiny comfort in a sea of pain. It was good though. All those tiny comforts add up.

"Thank you Jonathan for showing up and helping us through this ordeal. It's extremely hard not to feel like it was my fault. I'm really dealing with that. I just can't let go of the why? You know, I was made fun of as a kid. I'm sure you know that now, but for some reason I was ok. I know you think we would never have understood, but I would have. I really wish you would have talked to me about this. Maybe I couldn't have helped, but I could empathize. I did yell at you at times, got frustrated, but I loved you DEARLY. I put you in so many things to get you pumped up. I tried to let you be you. I loved the you! That's the hard thing about being 12. You don't understand that I was a kid too. I know your angels took you away. Of course you chose to stay. Who wouldn't? I can't wait to see you there!"

Going into month three, emotions are still all over the place and I am still living on an hour to hour basis. I have hatred for people I think hurt him. I want to hurt them. I am confused by the change in my friends. I am confused by the way they handle my grief. How am I supposed to act? I still want to talk about my son! It isn't fair! I just look at pictures and I see a beautiful soul. I miss him. I want to be someone he would be proud of, not a lump on the couch. Less than a month before he died my husband and I had toasted each other with a glass of wine so happy about the future. We kept saying we were going to be living "chapter two". We thought that chapter would include dinners at the new house, walks downtown, the kids closer to friends. I don't like the chapter I am living now at all. Some moments I am brave. I put on my happy face and meet someone for lunch. Then I feel sick, like I JUST WANT TO VOMIT OUT ALL THE

PAIN. Some days I don't even know where I'm at. I'm not totally depressed, but I'm just looking at an empty hole in front of me.

Mom,

I knew immediately it was a huge mistake. I don't even know why I did it really. It just happened. I thought 911 would save me. I could see you screaming and I was standing right next to you. I was telling you I was ok, but you didn't hear me. It was so noisy and chaotic, the angels took me away. They healed me and filled me with peace. I felt enormous and endless love. I knew you and Dad loved me so much. It's not like it wasn't enough, but I needed a different kind of love. I see that I would have gotten it later in life, but then I couldn't see it. Maybe I did have that kind of love in my life, but I didn't feel it at that exact moment. It's not ok, but it is ok. You just need to look ahead, look through the veil, and live your lives. I'm here for you all the time. Anytime. And it's beautiful here. I love you!

Jonathan

Moving on through month three is just like moving through mud. You have to get through all the mundane tasks. You get up. You get dressed. You work. You get gas. You pick up your daughter from school. You go home. You go to bed. The routine saved me. I was on autopilot.

We took another trip up north. One night we stayed in a historic hotel that reminded us exactly of the hotel in the movie, The Shining. We walked onto a vacant floor to find an empty ballroom and bar and we seriously felt like Jack Nicholson was going to come at us with an axe! Other than that, we had a pleasant evening watching the snow fall over the lake and chilled with our cheese plate and wine. Serenity now. It was good to get away. That was what saved us the first year. We live in a very busy 24/7 city that is oriented such that perfection is just the lowest standard. Up north, if you ask your waiter for a recommendation he might say, "You know, I just started here, but let me text my girlfriend she knows the menu well." Things are a little slower and people have the time to chat. I wished time would stop and we could take as long as we needed to heal without the added stress of life. But instead, things piled up. While we were away traveling and giving ourselves a break. the real world was still there breathing down our back.

The day before Jonathan would have turned 13, I was attacked by one of my patient's cats. I walked into his home and said hello. I sat down by the patient and turned towards a cat that was walking towards me when suddenly it hissed and jumped on my face. I really thought it was going to rip my face off. It was vicious and scarred my face and I do believe the cat saw you and you scared it. The medium did say the cats could see you. Yep the real world stops for no one.

We went to Morton's, your favorite restaurant for your birthday. I think that is something we will always do. I wish you would have been there for the steak and mashed potatoes. I miss you! I miss everything about you, but I especially miss your jokes. No one made me laugh as much as you! As we sat there, Jessica started to play with the oil lamp's wick and made the flame go up and down just like you and TJ did last year. Yes Jonathan, I will never forget THAT birthday, the night you almost burned the house down. Don't worry TJ, I'm not mad. It's a funny memory now.

We had taken Jonathan and his friend TJ to their favorite restaurant, Morton's. They were such foodies! When we got home from Morton's, I got out an old oil lamp I had so Jonathan and his friend could use it. We had it out for a bit and then I felt like they were getting a little careless with it so I put it away. Some time later my son came into the kitchen and got a glass of water. I asked why he needed the water and he said he was thirsty. That got me kind of suspicious because he rarely drank tap water. I followed him only to see our console and photos up in flames!! They had gotten the lamp out and they didn't light it properly and it blew up. Everything was fine, but yes. They had to play with fire. Typical life with Jonathan, aka Jano, as everyone else called him.

Keep the memories alive. Go to the places they liked. Talk about your loved ones. Write down everything you did. It might make you sad initially, but one day you will love reading them. You will love it all, the good and the bad.

Life continued. When I think back to that time, it's like I had a pick axe in my hand and I was climbing a mountain. Each hour I would put that axe in the mountain and lift myself to the next hour. Life did not have that flowing motion you see on the second hand of a clock. It was choppy. Sometimes my mind would just go someplace else and I would be completely unaware of time. I remember I would be thinking about Jonathan so deeply while driving, I would suddenly become aware that I had no idea where I was or how long I had been out of it. One of those times I was driving home from East Lansing and I was on a long stretch on the highway. I was in my trance like state and something made me snap back to reality. I looked up and saw a truck in front of me with a "big A". That made me think of another one of Jonathan's friends, Adam, because that was his user name, "bigA…". Right after I thought of that, I turned my head and there was a big billboard with "Livingston" on it. Adam Livingston. That is his name! My heart stopped. I had to pull over. Strong messages he always gives us!

Around this time, Adam was looking through youTube videos of a water park in Boyne. He had been there that summer and for some reason he just felt like looking at videos of the rides. He was watching a video of a girl waiting to go down this water shoot. The camera was on this girl's face for several minutes and then the camera turned around right into Jonathan's face! Then it showed him standing casually in line for about 10 seconds or so. He didn't know that girl, nor did we. The video was one out of thousands. Why did he watch THAT ONE? Unbelievable!

Another amazing sign happened right before Valentines day, my husband decided to give my son's lap top to his cousin. Before giving it away, my husband was looking through it and removing items that were private. He came across a Valentine Jonathan had made for us, but he had never given us. Inside a heart, he had written, "I love you because of the way you cook, I love the way you try to find spiritual peace, Sometimes when I get a bad grade, I feel like the world's going to end, but I know that you'll always love me, when you cook delicious food, it makes me feel happy, I remember all the days we act most loving, Valentine's day. And you filled my heart with love. You are loving, kind, and caring. And I love you because you are you." And I love you, Jonathan, because you are you. Thank you. I don't know of a better Valentine love note.

It was like this for a year, coincidences that weren't coincidences. I ask people who have loved ones that passed if they have received messages. So many have! Be open to them. Believe that it can happen! I was greedy for signs and dreams. They are what helped me get through the day. I often wondered how people grieved without the messages? It was so grateful for them! I guess it also helped that I read other people's experiences too. The first year, the dreams were so vivid and real and I thankfully dreamt of him several days a week. They were hard to wake from, but while I was dreaming they were SO wonderful!

I dreamt that I walked into the house and there you were sitting on your spot on the couch. I couldn't believe it! You had come back to life! We got a second chance. I held you and begged you not to get in trouble this time. I offered you one hundred dollars if we could make it through one year. Then it was the morning and you were walking with me and Jessica to the bus stop and while we were walking you saw a little boy with one of your toys playing in his yard. We gave away a lot of your toys and he had some of them. You ran up to him and wanted your toy back, but the boy ran into his house. You chased after him and so did I. I was telling you to leave him alone because I had given him the toy. I went into the house and was calling for you. I thought you were hiding from me and so I was looking for you behind the couch, under a table. The father awkwardly came up to me and asked me what I was doing? I said I was sorry, but my son ran into their house to get his toy from his son. He looked at me very sadly and told me that was not possible because my son was dead. I was so confused in my dream at that point. None of us had realized you were a ghost.

I woke up from that dream sad, but also happy that at least I saw you. I still remember what the hug felt like in my dream. I also felt like you were trying to tell us you still sat with us on the couch and watched TV with us. You still walked to the bus with Jessica. These were the small things I had to hold onto.

One thing I could not do during the first year was listen to music. It made me break down no matter what type of music it was. I drive from house to house making calls to my patients so I used to listen to music all day. It really got me through the day. After Jonathan died I no longer enjoyed it. My daughter was the opposite. Music was her therapy. For myself, it brought back too many memories and all the songs about love and relationships and feelings tore me up inside. It was hard to listen to the news also. All I could see was pain and misery in the world. Facebook was a place I could kind of vent and let some emotions out. My friends were very respectful of that and gave me space and support in expressing myself. On the flip side, it was hard to see my friends complain about their kids and how busy they were. I would have given anything to have that life back and I mean anything. I knew it was normal of them to complain, but it was hard for me just the same.

In between the sadness and pain was just sheer exhaustion. I would come home from work and lay down in bed. I read in bed, ate in bed, watched TV, talked on the phone, in bed. That reminds me of that Chinese fortune telling trick, say your fortune and then add "in bed" at the end. You will have great abundance in your life…in bed. I think I made an indentation on my side of the bed. It took me about 8 months to realize even if I didn't want to, I should go sit in different areas of the house. Imagine that I was too tired to get up from my bed and walk 15 feet to sit on my couch. I was too tired to interact with my family at dinner. There was a period that I allowed myself this habit. I felt like it was a normal part of grieving. After awhile I could see that if I didn't actively change this, it would become my life and so I forced myself to sit in other rooms, just to get up, just to move.

Around about this time I realized maybe the wine was getting out of hand. I had always had one or two glass of wine once a week. I noticed I was looking forward to occasions to drink more often and that I was drinking to numb my feelings. I can see why people self-medicate, because in that moment it works. Any relief from the crushing pain was welcome. I also could see that we have a shortage of mental health professionals. Most doctors are booked a month ahead when you call to make an appointment. A month is a long time to wait when you might need medication right away. Granted if you are suicidal you will get immediate help, but not for depression. So if you can't get help from a professional you might take matters into your own hands. The problem with self medicating is that it is ultimately destructive. I realized that although alcohol numbed my feelings, it is also a depressant. I was self medicating my depression with a depressant! Thankfully I was cognizant enough to know even a few months of this was dangerous and it had to end. It wasn't that I was getting drunk all the time. I drank just enough to make the pain bearable. I really needed to find healthy ways to deal with my depression. I already knew things that would help me. I just needed the energy to do them.

At some point it just becomes a choice. You must decide you are going to help yourself. It's not easy, in fact it is the hardest thing I have ever done because in a strange way pain had become my friend. Pain was Jonathan. If I let go of the pain, I let go of Jonathan. In the depths of my mind, the amount of pain I felt equaled the love I had for him. When I had glimmers of happiness in my life and I felt myself smile, I would instantly feel guilty. Even though I knew Jonathan would want me to be happy, I couldn't do it. Again I was somewhat aware this wasn't good for me, but it took almost two and a half years to finally put that notion to bed, to finally start living in the present and appreciate my family without Jonathan. In between that time I slowly worked on letting go. I analyzed those words, "letting go". What does that even mean? I imagined him floating away and me physically letting go of his hand. How could I do that? Well, I couldn't. So instead I lived in a world where emotions mashed up on each other and my goal was just to get through the day.

I was so thankful for my dreams. One night I dreamt we were just laying in bed watching TV and holding hands. I could feel the warmth of your body next to mine. You felt just the way you always did. I loved it! And then we looked up to the sky and saw fireworks. That was an A plus dream!

During this time I was still having these visions. I cannot imagine what or where they came from, but they definitely made me feel better. One day as I laid down and closed my eyes suddenly there was a butterfly with your eyes in it's wings. Every time I saw those visions it jolted me because it was as if I was seeing it right there in front of me except it was in my mind. I was told I was seeing with my third eye by spiritual people and that is what makes sense to me. Another time I saw you in a barber chair getting your hair cut. That really made me laugh! I want to emphasize these were not dreams. I was awake. If I closed my eyes a world opened up and I saw it in front of me like another reality. It was very very strange. It seemed that I was being guided to explore the spiritual world in order to heal and so I took that path.

I began doing guided meditations for grief that I found on YouTube. One that I found helpful was where the whole family sat on the beach and we just talked and we said our goodbyes and watched you walk off into a beautiful sunset. The mediation guides you into an appropriate conversation and encourages you to say the things you don't want to, like "goodbye". It was a peaceful way of starting the letting go process. Even though it would take years to do so, at least I was starting.

Walking in nature was my go to for a release. The very hard thing was that I had a minimal amount of energy so even though I knew it would help, it still was hard for me to get out and do it. My muscles had atrophied so much! I was out of breath walking a few blocks! However, on those occasions that I did get out, it was so good for me. I see God in nature, the way everything is just so perfect, and I feel joy in my heart to see such beauty. This is how I discovered how helpful photography was for me. I had begun photography as a hobby about a year before Jonathan died. It was an outlet for my creativity. I noticed that when I was focused on the other side on the lens I was able to stop thinking about how much I missed Jonathan. I put the focus outside of my head while I photograph. It also helps with anxiety I believe. Thus began my love affair with the camera. Another gift from the dead. Try it and see if while you are so focused on the different colors of a leaf and how the sunlight changes a red leaf to peach, you don't feel that stabbing pain anymore.

We went on our family spring break trip to the British Virgin Islands. We went with another family and rented a boat and sailed around the islands snorkeling and scuba diving. You had gotten certified the last summer. You were so looking forward to this trip. It was such a fun trip, but it was heart breaking just the same to be without you. We had a framed picture of you in the boat to make it feel like you were still there, even though we know you are always with us anyway. I brought one of your coins with me and I threw it in the ocean at the Bitter End Yacht Club. We had so much fun there the last time. Symbolic gestures were a big part of our lives back then. Everything had a meaning.

Of course we got strange messages there as well! My husband and his friend had gone on the same trip 19 years ago. They were sitting at the bar on this tiny island and his friend overheard a woman say she had been at the same bar exactly 19 years ago to the day. He looked closely at this woman and saw that it was the same woman they had gone with on their last trip with! My husband's old girlfriend decided to take the same trip at the same time that we did and we ended up on the same island on the same day! Coincidence or sign? Well, there is no such thing as coincidence in my opinion.

It was an amazing trip. The blue sea sparkled and the waves lulled us into a slumber. The underwater life and colors were fantastic! Another one of my loves is swimming, the underwater calm and the floating sensation brought me peace of mind. One day I followed a sea turtle for about an hour. When I closed my eyes at night I saw vivd sunsets. I knew you were telling me you with us in spirit, still I physically ached for you. I felt your presence so greatly that I kept thinking you would pop out from your hiding spot. That you would suddenly appear and tell me that the last few months had been a joke. We went to our restaurant, Pussers, and I looked at the table we sat at last time and it was all I could do not to burst into tears. The guys ate the foot long fried hot dog in your honor which was funny, but it would have been so much more entertaining with you there too.

The trip was a good escape. If possible, get away as much as you can. It was harder for us because Jonathan died in our back yard, so our house had all his living memories and it also had memories of his death. Our dog used to lay down on the spot he died in. Oh my. So much sobbing. Good to get away.

It was about seven months after his death. It still felt like a long life without him. If I think about it too much I feel like I will never make it, but I know I can make it one day.

He was so good at sending signs! I was looking for my taxes from the last year because I needed some information from them. I looked high and low for them, finally finding them in a cabinet in the garage. Looking through the stack I found the folder we used for Crime Busters, our activity in the Science Olympiad. That was such a great experience to be your team's coach! One of the exercises was to mix different items, like baking soda and vinegar and noting what happened. I guess extrapolating what this might mean in the real world would be able to identify substances found at a crime scene, like an explosion. We had so much fun mixing all those ingredients and watching to see what the reactions would be. I didn't really know what I was doing but I tried! It was very special to share that with you. I looked through the folder remembering the day we analyzed our finger prints. Then I went on Facebook and saw my memory. It was the day of the Science Olympiad! You wanted me to remember that day. Aw! I love you so much!

We decided to have a fundraiser in his honor. Doing good things for others always makes you feel better. Additionally, you might want to memorialize your child's name. Jonathan was a great lover of the outdoors and he had been to this particular camp three times, twice for summer camp and once for a school trip. He had a blast! It's always been so difficult for me to comprehend why we are so standardized in this country. Everyone must go to a public school and follow such strict rules and follow a common core. Jonathan was an out of the box thinker. He never fit into these guidelines and it caused him to be depressed at times. I so wish there had been a school for him to have more freedom and more time outside. I know education is complex and I don't mean to be negative, it's just that my son probably should have been homeschooled so we could have created a better learning environment for him. So I felt that as opposed to having something in the school I would put something at the camp. We had a fundraiser at a gymnastics facility where kids had an afternoon of open gym and the money went towards a climbing wall with Jonathan's name on it and to a scholarship for needy kids to get an opportunity to go to camp. I felt like he belonged at a fun place with kids where he could play with them. I imagined his spirit watching them climb his wall perched up at the top of a pine tree. Some people continue scholarships in their children's name forever. It might become their life's mission. I had mixed feelings after the fundraiser. I was happy and sad. Happy that we raised a lot of money for the kids. Sad that Jonathan was not there. I felt angry that the principal and vice principal were there. It was right that they were there, but it still made me angry. I still held them somewhat accountable. You were so unique. I loved that about you. I felt like I was surrounded by normal people now with normal thoughts. I was the odd ball with the dead son. All the other mothers had their kids with them. I just kept comparing the other kids to you and I thought I'll never have that quirky person making me look at life in a different way, your distinct way. Even though I was missing him I know raising money for kids to go to camp was a cause Jonathan approved of and he was right there in spirit jumping into the foam pit and swinging on the rope. I am so thankful for everyone that did show up. Jessica needed to know that people cared about Jonathan. My thoughts were varied at the event. I kept wondering what went wrong. I thought you could always stand up for yourself. I guess you did, but that lead to a detention. Was that the catalyst? I'll never know. Overall, it was an honor to raise money in his name and I did feel supported by the community.

The hard thing about losing a child is that it changes you so much. It changes your views. It changes your personality. It changes your politics. It changes your relationships. It changes everything. You realize how precious life is. You don't want to waste your time here on earth.

I am a practicing Podiatrist. I have been for 20 and some years. I chose this path for the stability and the ability to financially take care of my family. I have a creative side, but my family did not value that as I was growing up and I was deterred from taking a more artistic path. I have always had a small regret that I didn't have enough confidence in my abilities to find success in the arts. I also felt like it was a bit crazy to give up a lucrative job for a completely unknown life. I mean, it's not even like I had taken an art class since middle school. I dabbled in photography for my enjoyment, but could I make a job out of it? I'm a certified reflexologist too, but would I give up my extensive education to do this? Up until this point the answer would have been no, but losing Jonathan showed me that this was my only chance. This was my only chance to live a life I enjoyed. So I started creating my new life.

Part of this new life was working on my spirituality. I don't think there is actually an organized religion for my beliefs. I guess the foundation is Christian as I do believe in God and his words are so helpful and true. I don't take the bible literally though and I'm not a regular church goer. I know that will probably rub some of my readers the wrong way, but I am just being honest. My beliefs expand to thinking that there is another reality that is right next to ours and this is what we call heaven. We don't usually have access to this heaven, but those in heaven can have access to us. We are sent here to earth to learn lessons that enlighten us. We know before we leave heaven we will experience certain hardships and we except this because we know that these lessons will make us stronger and closer to God. While we are in heaven we know we will have other opportunities to come back and work on ourselves so it's easier to agree to live our lives with these difficulties. That might sound very bizarre to some people, but that is what I believe. And because of this despite the pain I feel, I know God gave me this hardship in order to develop compassion for others and to release my fear of making money. I am to find work helping others, but not to worry about how much money I make. I came to this notion through reading books on the afterlife, readings with mediums, meditation, massage, and long thinking. I am still working on making that life a reality, but I know that any day could be my last and I need to make these changes sooner than later.

And so, that changes relationships. I married a man that fell in love with a doctor with conservative ideas. He might not be so into a hippie healer. Thankfully I believe he is changing with me also. Perhaps he is changing to see that my dreams are valid or that he should make more money so I can stop worrying and quit my day job. That's still in progress, but I think you get my drift.

My sister and I took our daughters to Sedona. As you can clearly see. I really needed to get away that first year! We felt like we needed the energy provided by the vortexes and the mind set of the people there. My daughter was a little bummed out about Sedona, preferring something flashy like New York City but I knew she would not only love it, but she would find a piece of herself there. I remember our drive from Phoenix to Sedona. The scenery starts out a little scratchy and dry, but then the desert landscape transitions into the mountains, canyons, and bright green, almost neon green, trees. The green and orange colors are so vivid it takes your breath away. I remember driving by Red Rock and the kids had to get out of the car in wonder. Mom made an excellent choice.

We started the trip with Jerome, a historic ghost town. What a great little spot! We started at the top of the hill at a hotel and restaurant called Asylum Restaurant. It was a renovated asylum. There were a few remnants that gave you that slightly creepy crazy feeling, but other than that it was beautiful, situated in the rocks and had a great view of the city below. The streets zig zag down to the bottom of the hill and there are lots of cool shops and historic sites, such as an original jail cell. One store that we loved was Nellie Bly Kaleidoscope store. We were told we had to go there and truthfully I wasn't that interested, but we went there anyway. That ended up being one of my favorite stores. There were so many kaleidoscopes in every size and it's so fun to see the desert distorted in so many ways. I really did not know who Nellie Bly was. We learned she was a journalist who did an expose on the insane asylums, blowing their cover as inhumane and she also decided do around the world in 80 days and made it in 72. She was quite a woman! Strangely a few days after we came back, all over Facebook there were suggested posts on Nellie Bly. It was Nellie Bly Day and my nephew had to do a report on her! We had never heard of her and suddenly her name and face was everywhere! Weird.

We did a lot of hiking while we were there. Just unbelievable views and the feeling it gave me, oh. I wished I could just travel and hike every day for the rest of my life. My daughter also shares a love of nature, but it had previously been more about the aesthetics and not the healing benefits. That is something she can carry with her forever, that in times of stress nature will nurture you. Another popular site is the Chapel in the Rock. I had been to Sedona several years ago and I had forgone this tourist spot because I felt it was a little too touristy, but this time I felt like it might be good for me. We went there and stood in line to get into the Chapel. It's magnificent, built right into a rock and there is a back window that is from the floor to ceiling that overlooks Sedona. I went in and sat down and said a prayer. I prayed for help and guidance and strength. I felt a peace wash over me and in that moment I felt right. Of course it did not last, but when I was able to even feel moment of relief it gave me hope. Hope that maybe that moment of peace could turn into an hour, an hour into a day.

That night when I walked into our room the lights clicked off. Ok that could happen to anyone! Then, an hour later, my daughter walked in and the lights clicked on. Ok a little weird. I had one of my dreams

that night. I dreamt that I was at a swim meet and on one side, the side with the swim starters were the stands, on the other side was a stage and there were yoga mats piled up. I was sitting atop the yoga mats as I thought it was a better view when suddenly all the yoga mats slid off into the pool with me on them! This happened during an event with the swimmers in the pool! Every one was so mad at me because they had to redo the event and some of the swimmers felt it ruined their chances for a state cut. I went into the stands and was sitting there alone and wet. The parents of the swimmers were giving me looks of disgust. I felt very awkward and guilty and was thinking about leaving when in walked a man. He was about 27-30. He was dressed in a natural, casual outfit, with shoulder length wavy brown hair. He looked like a rugged guy from Colorado. He was good looking enough, but he had the most beautiful blue green eyes and a dazzling smile. It was as if rays of sunshine came out of his mouth when he smiled. He sat down next to me and started to laugh, like boy you really blew that one! I appreciated his humor and it lightened my mood. He asked me how I was doing? I told him I was doing ok. He thought ok didn't sound very good and so we started to talk about how feeling ok could be turned into feeling great. He told me I needed to go to church. I said I did and made him laugh. No I was adamant, I did go to church. Well, he said, you go to church and you listen, but you don't really hear God's words. True, I might be guilty of that. He said I needed to start hearing instead of listening. He told me to fill my life with goodness, such as honesty, charity, friendship. He also said that when terrible things do happen just to accept them as they are. That time will pass and the problems will be dealt with and we won't even barely remember them. We talked about those things for awhile and then he looked at me and smiled and said he I would be fine and patted me on the knee. Then he walked out the door with a wave. When I awoke I felt like I had talked to Jesus. It could have been just a cute guy in my dreams, but my feeling is that it was Jesus. As I awakened from my dream I saw the vivid streams of color in my mind and your face. It was clear you had sent that message to me in my dream. My prayers made in the chapel had been answered.

The rest of the trip was beautiful and a lot of fun. We took a hike to Buddha Beach at Crescent Moon State Park where there are thousands of rock towers made by people passing by. We each made one also. I guess we all had our thoughts in our own minds why we built ours, but I built mine with the hopes of finding a new balance in my life. The idea of learning to balance the rocks would help me learn to balance my emotions. My sister had a few spiritual happenings in Sedona also, but those are her stories to tell.

So it was back to reality, I had been handed a few more tools to help me through this misery, but even though you have the tools you still need to know how to use them and you have to remember that you do have them! So much easier to lie in bed as opposed to getting out there and and doing something like walking for breast cancer.

It is always hard to come back from vacation. We always wish they were longer. It's bad enough to come back to bills and jobs, but to come back to and feel the depression bleed back into your mind and body is dreadful. Can I keep living my life like this day after day only to escape the pain by physically running off to a vacation spot? Getting through the day is surviving and that IS important, but I wanted more. I had to get real with myself. How am I going to live? I looked over at my back pack of tools sitting there in the corner and

then picked it up. I took the tools out and looked at them one by one wondering what I would do with them? Then I started to work on myself. I started to walk more to get my energy levels up. I met friends for coffee. I stopped isolating myself in the house. I continued meditation. I went to my daughters school functions. I shared my stories on the after life with grieving patients. I started to move. I started. Not going to lie. I was crying silently in the car so many times before an event and had to pray to pull myself together. So many lunches I forced myself to go, but I did it.

A few days before Mother's day, I was getting my eyebrows done. The woman that did my eyebrows asked me if I was excited about Mother's Day? I said I guess so? She told me this Mother's Day was going to be hard for her because she lost her 4 month old son this year. Then she told me about a dream she had where his coffin was lifted up to the sky. I told her about my son and we gave each other a hug and wished each other a peaceful Mother's Day.

Mother's Day came, another of my favorite holidays! I tried so hard to be a good mother. I tried 110 percent, like I said before. I was not one of those super helicopter moms cutting sandwiches into stars. I was just trying to raise my kids in a healthy, loving environment and I pushed myself everyday to be there for them and be a good role model. We laughed so much. I remember so many times laughing so hard I almost threw up. Jessica was the one with the funny faces and would dress up weirdly. Jonathan had the funny stories and songs. People might think we were nuts, but we got each other. I remember once when Jonathan was in the fourth grade we went to his music concert. He didn't sing one word he was mouthing them, but he was overdoing it and making weird faces like he was a rapper and whatever arm motions they had, he would put a twist on them like they were gang signals. Jon and I were in tears of laughter practically falling off our seats. I don't think anyone else thought it was that funny. I loved Mother's Day. A whole day to be treated like a queen and be appreciated. That first year was not the same. We went through the motions, but it was very sad. I feel so bad for Jessica because she must have felt not enough. She was still here. I'm still a mom. I should be happy for what I did still have, but all I could see was what I didn't have, Jonathan.

It was late at night on Mother's Day that I drove over to my Mom's. There was a light spring rain that brought out the scents of the blooms. I drove by a patch of lilac trees and thought spring has come, my favorite season, and the lilacs are in full bloom and I barely even noticed. I felt like I should pull over and smell the lilacs, but then thought that was a weird idea. I went over to my mom's place and it was rough. I mean I could barely talk and I only stayed for a few minutes just for a hug and to give her a card. On the way back I decided to stop by the lilacs. I just stood by the bushes and breathed in the scents. Ah, things started to slow down. The tears slowly stopped, my breathing not so ragged, my heart stopped racing. I pulled a branch off to take home and I heard Jonathan say, "I love you, Mommy." Mother's Day completed. He wanted me to notice my favorite bloom and he gave me a flowering branch to take home with me.

We got an offer on our house. We didn't even have it on the market, but a friend of a friend was looking for a ranch house in our area. It sold! I have to say that moving out of that house might have been one of the worst experiences of my life, on par with his funeral. Packing up the house was dreadful. My God, 17 years of belongings. I still had my clothes from when we got married. I had saved my dresses from the engagement party and rehearsal dinner. Looking at them reminded me of those young flirty, hopeful days. The linen closet was filled with their beach toys. We had a whole closet filled with crafts, games, and their old projects. Sorting through the memories was good, but heartbreaking. We saved his room for last. We hadn't touched it since the day he died. His laundry was still in his basket. His homework and books in his backpack by his bed. There were loads and loads of toys to be thrown out. So many legos and little action figures that were at the bottom of his chest. I saved about 25 of his favorite lego guys. I could hear his voice in my head saying it was a rare one and not to throw it out. I found an old test he had gotten a perfect score on. Why hadn't we celebrated that? I remember I had given him a high five for that. I should have have hugged him tight and really made him feel special for that. I found his Michindoh Camp book. He had won the contest for the design on the cover. I remembered Jessica guiding him on the book and how much time he spent on it. I found a wallet that had been made out of duct tape with a cow on it. He was so good at saving money. I was sobbing for hours trying to get it packed. I was sobbing while I was packing. And all during this a Pirates of the Caribbean toy that had a pirates voice was going off. I had to wonder if Jonathan was behind that! I found a bag of rocks. I felt maybe they should stay with the house so I took them out and was randomly tossing them out in the back of the house. The last rock in the bag I was about to throw, but then I looked at it. Jonathan had drawn a face on it, a smiley face. I kept that one! That was definitely a sign. He was happy for us. The move was a good thing.

We moved into my Mom's condo and she moved in with my sister. It feels a little weird because it's not our space. It's my mom's and we are just here. I feel numb. I feel like this is something happening to someone else. I feel sad. I feel exhausted. I am hoping it all works out. I am hoping this radical change will be good for us. It just doesn't seem fair. Again, I'm still holding onto you.

I dreamt that I was in my office and the phone rang and it was you on the line! You told me I had to be nicer to Daddy or I would lose him. I will, I promise…

I was feeling very sad, those days and weeks after the move. Ok let's be honest months after the move I was still very depressed. I felt like maybe I just need to feel it. I need to stop fighting the sadness and denying it and just live in the sadness. So I did for awhile. I found that sadness refuses to just go away. It sits outside the door waiting for you and insists on being felt.

I was in my Mom's room, currently my room, and I was scanning her bookshelves. It wasn't like I was actually going to read something, it was just something to do. I found my seventh grade yearbook. I hadn't seen that probably since I had graduated from high school. I opened it up and started to leaf through it. The memories started to flood back. How humiliated I was when Peter snapped my bra strap. I could actually feel my cheeks burning in shame and the feeling of not being able to stand up for myself. Then there was the time I was picked last for gym and I almost felt like I couldn't go back to school the next day. It was hard not to be popular. It was hard keeping my grades up. It was hard when friends ditched me. But every year got better, Jonathan. By the time I was 18 it was totally different. You were transforming before my eyes, Jonathan. Girls were going to fall for those blue eyes! I do believe I found that yearbook so I could relive what a 12 year old goes through. So I could connect with what Jonathan might have been feeling before he died. It was so hard to believe his problems lead to his death. I thought it had to be something bigger, something really bad, like maybe I didn't love him enough. But I was able to see that maybe something that I considered small, was enough to push a person's button, especially a 12 year old that has no perspective on life yet. And I also realized by looking at my yearbook how important my peers were. How much they dominated my thoughts. The love of my parents was taken for granted.

I dreamt we were at a family party at Uncle Scott's house. We were in the kitchen having a good ole time. I decided I needed some alone time so I went off and went down a hall. Suddenly I was in my childhood bedroom. I was sitting on the floor in darkness but looking up at the top bunk where I used to sleep. Then in front of me I saw some legs and I looked up and saw khaki shorts, your khaki shorts! It was you! You weren't whole like a person, but you weren't transparent. You sat down in my lap and I hugged you. You felt like you, but there was also an energy surrounding you that made me tingle. We hugged each other and I could feel the love between us. I looked into your eyes and we connected, a mother and a child. Then you slowly disappeared. I woke up and my arms were still tingling.

You tried so hard to help us! You really wanted us to know you were ok. You gave us dream after dream, sign after sign. I knew you were ok, but that still didn't keep me from desperately missing you.

We went to the medium again. This time my husband, Jon, went to. It was also a good connection, but this time Jon's mom and dad contacted us and not as much Jonathan. It was a good reading, but I felt like Jon's resistance and lack of enthusiasm kind of blocked the energy.

Slowly I was starting to get adjusted to the move. We had moved to a condo right in a downtown area with shops and restaurants around us. Living in a downtown atmosphere was helpful for me. I am an extrovert so I did like getting up with the dog for a walk and seeing people. I didn't know them. It was just good to see people and be out in the world. I enjoyed walking for a cup of coffee and the mild exercise was good for me. Unfortunately as the sadness faded, the other emotions ran in and overwhelmed me! While I was sad and in a fog, I was kind of a peaceful loving person. When I wasn't feeling sad and foggy, I started to feel angry and irritable! Everyone was amazed at how gracefully I handled Jonathan's death and I guess compared to some maybe I did. But I did not feel graceful. Where previously I had been on the bottom of the ocean and unaware of the world outside, I was now on the surface of the ocean treading, fighting the waves, sometimes going under the water, sometimes floating. I snapped at people. I didn't care about other people's problems. Sometimes I did care. I cared too much. I felt extreme pain for mothers on the news searching for a missing child. I wanted to help troubled children. I wanted to save them. Everything that was going on, I felt it more. I felt like people were being ridiculous about politics. Who cares? We're all going to die.

This is when things started to get a little difficult between my husband and I. On days where I was doing better, that made him mad. Didn't I love my son? On those days he would yell at me for no reason and where as before I might have understood he was just sad, I started to yell back at him. We really had never been the fighting couple. Our relationship was pretty easy, maybe boring at times. Now we couldn't stop. My daughter hated this. She started isolating herself. However, this is just something we had to go through. Just like we had to deal with the sadness we had to deal with the anger. We just had to let it out or we would explode. Father's day was worse than Mother's day. All my husband wanted to do was go to my son's grave and he was extra snappy all day. This of course made my daughter really sad because she had planned a dinner for him. Again, she was left feeling not enough. Of course that was the opposite. She was cherished beyond words. That's just not how she felt. So the next day we talked about how we could let off steam without yelling at each other and we did. We couldn't help feeling angry, but we didn't need to use each other for punching bags.

My husband went to a few therapy sessions and although he didn't follow it through until the end he did gain some skills to get him through the moment. He's not the talking type and he felt like it was doing more harm to sit there and talk about it. That was hard for me because I was trying anything to get better, but his philosophy was that it would just get better with time. I think time does help, but to convince him he needed more than that was difficult. Thankfully, he loved me enough to know that he didn't want to lose me. He knew he needed to change.

Summer came. Normally, I loved summer because we didn't have the stress of so many school activities and there was no homework to contend with. And let's be honest, who doesn't need a few months of sun after a cold Michigan winter? I also got to spend more time with them. As a working mom I always missed them. We were quite active in the summer. On my days off I took them on excursions and we explored different cities around the state. They were on a summer swim club and had lots of friends there. We wake boarded on the lake, took trips up north, slept in, and just enjoyed being with family. I was one of those moms that wanted the summer to never end. This year I missed him at the swim meets. When the 13-14 boys swam I had to hold back my tears. Didn't he know how proud I was of him going to all those morning practices and every meet and giving his all? He felt like his sister was better than him at everything, but that was just because she was older. I felt so self conscious at the pool too, like all the moms were staring at me. I didn't have to buy you golf shirts. No more golf. The instructor said you had the best swing. I thought you might be on the golf team in high school. It was really weird to not have the babysitter tell me all the trouble you got in every day. I never thought I would miss that! This summer, I just went through the motions. Remember, it's the mundane tasks that will get you through the day. Don't discount that. It's really a feat to get through the day while grieving.

We didn't completely blow off the summer. We did have some good times. We went kayaking a few times. We went strawberry picking. We went up north. We tried to get used to being on vacations without you and it wasn't easy. It's hard to have fun when you are trying so hard to have fun.

Jessica did a few fundraisers. She did The Color Run and The Motor City Mile that summer. She enjoyed the physical challenge and it does help to feel like you are helping others. I think the most important thing is to find a cause you are really passionate about.

I went from feeling sad and depressed to angry to empty. I was trying so hard to get better, but failing. I would have several very depressed days. Those days I didn't take showers, I rolled out of bed sometimes going to work in the clothes I wore the day before and had slept in. Yeah, that's right I did. I forgot where I was going all day. I got pulled over for turning on red lights and stopping at a green light. I literally was not aware. Those days were almost better that the endless empty days. I call it emotional flatlining. I didn't exactly feel sad, but I wasn't happy. I didn't even feel numb. At least numb is a feeling. I felt nothing. So when I tried to do fun things to bring up my spirits it didn't even help. At first I didn't mind because I thought it was better than feeling pain, but eventually I could see that this wasn't good either. I remembered in my mind what it felt like to climb up to the top of a hilltop and look down at a beautiful view. I thought maybe if I did something like this, something that had made me so happy in the past, I would feel better. I put my hiking shoes on and found the nearest hill to climb. I huffed and puffed to the top only to feel nothing but disappointed. There was a beautiful view and I could SEE that it was beautiful, but I FELT nothing. I stayed this way for a long time.

I practiced writing down my feelings and trying to have a different perspective about them. For example, as I drove down the street and passed the school I would start to get a horrible feeling in my heart. So I wrote down in my journal, "seeing the school makes me angry because I feel like something at school hurt my son and the principal did not handle it appropriately." Then next to that statement I wrote, "seeing the school makes me angry because I feel like something at school hurt my son and the principal did not handle it appropriately, but he was just following rules and he didn't know just as no one knew what would happen next." I started journaling my feelings and tried to change them into feelings that were a little less exaggerated and distorted. "I am annoyed that my friend didn't check on me' became "I am annoyed that my friend didn't check on me, but she's just awkward not thoughtless." After doing this regularly I was able to stabilize my anger and sadness and not feel overwhelmed by them. I didn't have to feel so abandoned by the friend that never checked up on me. I mean, she just couldn't handle it. She's human. So I could let go of that annoying feeling of abandonment. I could let go of hating the principal. He was just doing his job the way he was trained. This may seem small to my readers, but it was miraculous to me. I spent a lot of time burning up thinking about that detention and what happened? And really, what was the point? How was burning up in anger going to help me? By forcing myself to try to understand another's perspective and then writing it down in black and white, I started to accept it. It was like seeing it was believing it. And by writing them down, I was able to release them from my thoughts because I could just reread them if I needed to. I didn't have to endlessly dwell on them.

I also played this game that helped to stop the inner loop of depressing conversation in my head of the things that day that had gone well, even if it was as small as having a good cup of coffee. Sometimes that would transition into a different internal conversation about coffee in my brain just long enough to distract myself from the depression. This trick worked in two ways. It forced me to see that there were still good things happening in my life and it distracted me from my depressing thoughts.

I would kind of pick and choose what days I would allow myself to wallow in sadness and wear my bathrobe and what days I would force myself to get up and actively work on healing. Some days the wallowing is healing and sometimes it's the moving that is healing.

I had a dream that you and I were in a room and you were telling me what happened. I don't know if this is really true, but you said that someone made fun of an Instagram post and you were VERY upset about that! I tried to tell you it was not a big deal. I tried to understand how upset you were, but I didn't get it. In the end we just had to agree to disagree and be happy to see each other.

This is a weird thing. When people ask how my family is, I actually think of you as alive, but you have the "dead disease". My mind still cannot process that you are gone. I understand how a broken heart can kill you now. I will be fine, but I will never be the same.

I had a dream that you and Max were playing and having such a fun time. I miss that smile. I miss your laugh. Still walking that long road.

I had a dream you gave Dad a bigggg hug. You just laid on his lap and hugged him. That was a good one!

I had a dream you were a baby and you were sleeping next to me, then I went to the bathroom and you were gone. I was screaming for you, then I noticed a bump under the covers and then you started to crawl and I knew you were going to go over the edge of the bed and I screamed for you to stop but you didn't and fell. Then you were crying and I picked you up and comforted you and you smiled.

How typical. You were always hiding from me. When Jonathan was about two, we were running errands. It was always such a chore with him because he loved to run down the aisles. I am sure everyone looking on thought I was the crazy mom that lets her kids do anything, but I had learned there was just no way to stop him, and why not run free as long as he didn't hurt anyone. Of course I was keeping an eye to make sure he didn't get out of control. One day, we went to pick up the dry cleaning. There was a parking space right in front of the store, literally a few feet away from the door. I parked and told Jonathan not to move. I went into the cleaners and I watched the van. A few minutes later I had my laundry and got into the van. I looked back at you and you were gone! I let out a yelp of fear! Where did you go? Then you popped up your head and giggled, "here I am!". Yes that was you, I told you not to move and you had to. You had to play a trick on me.

I have to accept that everyday I will miss him. I wish I could have helped him. I wish I would have known anything. I wish I was there that day. I wish you still had still been going to football practice. I wish.

I still can't answer that question, "How many kids do you have?" I still think I have two. I still will never talk about your death because I can hardly believe it. I still expect you to be on the couch after school. I still expect you to be in the car behind me. I'm having a bad day. I'm really disappointed in some people not being there for me. I can't believe I never even got one text to check on me and ask how I am doing! I'm really struggling with the why. I'm not joking when I say I tried 110 percent to give my all. I wasn't perfect. No. I was way better than I ever thought I would be. God please give me strength. Please support my family. Please help me be a better person. Please let me see Jonathan again.

The grind goes on. No one is special enough to stop it. While I am trapped in this awful place, people just go on about their lives without a worry. It's not fair. They just expect you to get on with life, which we are, but it's so challenging. The A finals for swimming is tomorrow. I remember buying his fast skin last year. He took 4 seconds off his 100 back. I was really proud of you. I took so much pleasure in watching you in the parade before the meet. You were supposed to be Minions. I remember how funny we both thought the yellow body paint was! I loved how much you got into the spirit. I miss you so much. He keeps telling me I still have Jessica. I still have Jessica.

You said it wasn't our fault. That you were being bullied. You were upset about a girl. That's what the medium told us you said. You were too dramatic. I can't help thinking about what I could have done to change things. I had a dream last night and you were about three and I looked right into your blue eyes and I thought how lucky I was to have you. I felt our connection. Then you wanted to show me a little mouse that you had dissected. Very strange that you showed me that. It made me question all the times I didn't have time for you and made me feel sad.

Dear Jonathan,

You are in my thoughts everyday. You know that right? When I walked along the shoreline at Lake Huron, I saw spots that I know you would have loved. Birmingham was not the place for you. You would have loved to live in the country. I could never have imagined having a child like you. I didn't appreciate the country as a child! I do understand not fitting in though. I don't even know if that was the issue, whether you fit in or not? I know you wanted more playdates. You weren't invited to that many parties. Your interaction with kids could be difficult. Everyone always loved your humor and kindness though. I'm greedy. Please keep giving me signs and dreams. I know you can! I also know you need to be free though. Can we compromise? Love you buddy! Have a good day!

Mom

Dear Mom,

I am so sorry! So very sorry! More than you can imagine. I just need you to forgive me so I can move forward. I love you, Dad, and Jessica so much! I wish I didn't hurt you. I am with you on every adventure and I want you to have so many more. Unfortunately your life is not about being a mother, but a healer and you need to face your fear of not being financially secure and be the person you are meant to be once and for all. You say you are lost, but that is not true. You are afraid. Please, Mom, let go. This is your chance. We will see each other again. There will be more dreams. You will learn how to connect with me as you develop your intuition. I love you Mom. Miss you. See you soon!

Jonathan

Those Facebook memories are a blessing and a curse. I opened up Facebook and there was your smiling face holding a fish from Alaska, one year ago. That happy happy face! I quickly scrolled past that as my heart lurched into my stomach. How dare Facebook keep bringing up memories that make me sad! Ok and two more times I opened up Facebook to that post. Ok I get it. Sometimes I am dense. He wanted me to remember him happy. He wants me to remember the good times. I'll try!

Finally another dream with you in it! You wanted to hang out with your football team. Whatever the reason, I was happy to see your face if only in my dreams!

So the summer past in kind of a blur. The school year started without you. I didn't have two kids in my back to school Facebook post. I'm feeling odd right now. I can't believe so much time has past, that I have made it this far, yet it seems like yesterday you were still with us. It's like a wrinkle in time to me. Some days are getting better though. It's not like I'm on the bottom of the ocean or even struggling to stay at the surface. I'm just tired. Tired of treading water everyday. Thankfully occasionally a wave carries me and I am bodysurfing instead of treading. That's a good feeling. I would be grateful if a boat found me and picked me up though.

My passion in photography continued to develop. This was probably the best therapy for me, finding a passion. It was amazing to actually enjoy small moments in life. My goal was to everyday find something beautiful and take a picture of it. If I can see beauty, I can believe it still exists. Many of our summer days consisted of photo shoots. Still one of my favorite things to do is sit down and edit my photos. I love expressing my feelings through photography. It's hard for me to describe how painful the grief is, but I can show you.

I was reading a lot. I found it to be very soothing and distracting. Reading about other survivors always made me feel hopeful I could be one too. I especially liked reading about people who had near death experiences and had visions of being in heaven or about people who had experiences seeing their departed loved ones. I had had so many visions, dreams, voices, it really helped to have them verified by others.

One night I was up very late reading The Hand on The Mirror. In it, the writer describes some pretty weird stuff that happened to her. In part of the book she says that we must ask our guides and deceased to give us messages. We must be open to them. I felt like I was very open and I asked for signs all the time. I didn't always get the signs or dreams when I asked for them. It just seemed random, like I got them when I got them not just when I asked. That night I said to my guides, "Ok. Give it to me. I'm ready for anything. Hit me with something REALLY good tonight!" I read for a little more and then I decided even though it was 6 am I should at least try to get an hour of rest. I put my Ipad down and I got comfortable in bed and closed my eyes. Within minutes I was not in my body. I WAS in my bed, but I had traveled somehow to someone elses back porch. I had instantly gone from lying in my bed to lying on a porch. I could feel the early morning air on my face. I could feel the dew on the grass. I was touching my face and the ground to see if I was still there in one piece and was this real? Yes, I was. I was looking up into the sky and wondered if I had been drugged. Did I sleep walk? I felt for my phone but I didn't have it. I guessed I would have to walk. I struggled from a sleeping position to an upright one and tried to stand up, but I fell towards the cement and as my face was getting close to hitting it I thought, "this is going to hurt". Instead of hitting the cement though I went through it like butter. I didn't feel a thing! I was suddenly floating in a luminescent light that was whitish lavender. I was me, but without a body, but I was me. I floated along for what seemed like five minutes. Enough time for me to feel like what it was like to exist as an energy and not as a body and to still feel whole. Then I saw Jonathan's eyes. We communicated without talking and I understood. I am not my body. I am my soul. My soul lives in a body. This world that I live in is not reality. It is a reality. The realities are so close together they exist within each other. I got it. I understand now. And then I woke up.

This is the most profound and life changing event I have ever had. I feel like I could actually write a book about this experience, but for now you just need to know it happened. There isn't a word to describe how I felt. I was freaked out to say the least, but at peace too. I don't have to like that I live this life without Jonathan, but I do know his spirit is right with us. I do know that life goes on beyond the physical. We think of "heaven" as something above us, but it actually surrounds us. The spiritual world vibrates at a higher frequency so we don't see it, but it's here. There are occasions where the frequencies meet and we can communicate and that is what I experienced. I was instructed to ask for this and I was completely open and wanted something like this to really, beyond a doubt, finally convince me that all the signs, dreams, visions were real connections. It had to be something really really big. I'm laughing as I write this as if I hadn't already had complete proof. That just shows you how stubborn I am! To my readers, you may be thinking this is pure craziness, but it did happen to me and whether anyone believes me or not it was sublime and oh so wonderful.

Another night I woke up and as usual, it was always a blow to realize again my son was dead. Moments after I woke up I had a vision of Jonathan's eye staring at me. Then he climbed out of the pupil and sat down on the lower edge of his eye and waved at me. It was just as clear as if I saw it in real life, but it was in my mind, my third eye. I still am amazed by this! How does this happen? I don't know. I just know that it can. I can still feel his energy and at least there is that. I do hope that my readers can find solace in my experiences. They are with us!

These events would buoy me through the next year. It was still hard to control the emotions. I felt every emotion all day long. One second I felt like I was going to be ok, only to have a flash of anger jolt through me and next a feeling a desolation. I would try to tell myself to make those feelings go away, but at this stage they were too powerful. Jonathan was a very very strong personality. I still have yet to meet anyone like him. It's hard to stop that eternal missing. I had true peace that he was ok. I fully understood we would meet again. But I still wanted him now. I didn't want to be changed. I didn't want to face my fears. I just wanted everything to be the way it was. Then I would remember my out of body experience and I would realize it had to be this way. Things had to change. I was meant to have these lessons and I slowly became more accepting, stronger. That strength carried me to get on with my work with a better attitude and focus on Jessica and Jon more. We were starting to get back to a normal family dynamic, not feeling the hole where he once lived quite so much. I was starting to appreciate what I did still have in my life and trying to show my family that I loved them. I was starting to actually care about things again, just a glimmer, but better. Still there were bad moments.

There were lots of bad moments. At this point we were mostly on our own. It's not that people didn't care or want to support us. It's just the way it is. I would encourage people to continue their prayers and to keep stopping by, texting or calling if they know someone that has lost a close loved one. I needed support badly, but I understood people had their problems and life too. If you are thinking of helping though, it's never too late. Most people think support is needed the most in the beginning and everyone sends cards and food, but it's after the ragged and endless months have gone on that a person could really use a boost.

I was not taking care of myself, truthfully I'm still not that great. I think I sometimes hated myself. When you don't love yourself, it's hard to love others and my family needed me. I needed a whole lot of loving! I thankfully am very aware of what I am feeling and eventually do try and fix things. I haven't been able to consistently love and take care of myself but I do more than I don't now. Part of that is taking a shower and putting on make up. I can't tell you how much I hated to do this. I guess I liked feeling as ugly on the outside as I did on the inside. Again, I knew this wasn't good for me, but some days I didn't care. Truthfully, I should say most days.

I added self love and forgiveness to my journaling. It was always a relief to get my thoughts out of my head even if it was only temporary. What do I love about myself? Well I love that I am able to see humor in dark moments. I love that I am a prompt person. I love that I am a good listener. I love that I am trying to change my life for the better. I love that I am a tree hugger. I guess I do love myself. I guess it does feel good to put my best person out there and interact with the world. I guess the world does need me. Forgiving myself was a little harder. I just felt like I should have known. I'm not a mind reader though. How could I know what was in my son's head if he was hiding it from me? I'm not a fortune teller either. How could I know that day would be any other than the last? I couldn't. It's still a leap to really think this was meant to happen, but years later when my daughter was dealing with depression and suicidal thoughts, the signs were so obvious! She crashed her car. She was caught drinking. She was slamming doors and isolating herself. Of course she needed therapy and she did get the help. She is here on earth supporting other teens through depression through her writing and through social media. She is meant to stay. These are the things I processed while journaling all the while trying to stay conscious of writing my thoughts in a way that was loving and compassionate towards myself.

In the moments where I was writing I was able to feel some relief, but most of the time I still felt the heavy thick blanket of pain surrounding me and it frustrated me because I didn't want to feel that way. I remember feeling that I wasn't doing enough to get better. I felt guilty that I hadn't joined a support group. I compared myself to others and thought I should work out more. I'd feel better if I had a kick ass body! So why wasn't I doing these things? I'm not much of a bible reader, but our minister had given me a book, called Jesus Calling, by Sarah Young. There are daily devotionals to read in times of need or just for inspiration. I pulled out the book and read the page of the day, October 10. It said to trust Him to let things happen without trying to control or predict them. We are to live fully in the present, depending on Him each moment. It is a sin to think we are more powerful than Him.

That was just what I needed to hear. I didn't need to beat myself up. I just had to trust that I would be ok in time. I had to be grateful that at least I felt freedom while I was writing or out in nature taking photos. I just had to trust that I would find the right therapist at the right time when I was ready. I had to trust that my business would take off when I was mentally capable of handling it. My life would return to normal when I was ready. I just needed to relax and have faith.

I muddled along having a variety of days, but I had a real set back in the fall. For a solid month at least every day was a bad one. The lead up to the day you died was torture. I relived the days we had spent together the year before and wondered why hadn't I seen it coming. I remembered a particular tree on the street that we both had admired and you told me NOT to take a picture of it. I did. I looked at that picture and I could still hear you saying, "MOM!" when I laid down in the street to get a good angle. I remember seeing the new house for the first time together. You were waiting on the steps for me to get there. It was love at first sight and you and Jessica ran through the house picking your rooms. You made plans with TJ for the summer. You would be able to ride your bikes to each other's house. You were going to be the first one to sleep in the house after we closed on the new house. They weren't all good memories. You were mad on Halloween. You didn't have anyone to go trick or treating with. You were mad that you missed the Harlan Frolic. I thought about the detention.

Every memory from the year before came back to me. It was like my current life was superimposed on my old life, but with a warped perspective because as I lived each day this year you were missing from it. I was acutely aware of the scenery being the same, but I had changed. I had been so happy. Now I am drenched in sadness. I used to feel hopeful and optimistic. Now I just hoped to get by. Some changes were better, like not caring about the small stuff or appreciating life more, but I wasn't really feeling the good changes at that time. People started to post football pictures on Facebook and I missed watching you play so bad. I remembered your last football game. I remember our conversation as we walked out, you thought it was funny I didn't know you had to ride back to school in the bus, silly mom. I tried to get you to just ride home with me. Why didn't I cherish that moment? Why didn't I give you a great big hug? Why didn't we go get ice cream when you got good grades on your report card? I remembered the change in the air, that little nip, that had made me excited about life. That same nip was the one I felt in my hands as I shook you hoping to bring you back to life. How different I felt one year ago. I was a different person. I remembered that beautiful day I came home and my life changed forever. I was robbed of your future. I saw your classmates getting older, but you would always be 12, every year.

Those were rough days, November 13th being the worst, but I made it. It was a milestone. I don't know why that day would be any worse than the others we suffered through, but it was. I remember Jessica, Jon and I got into a huge fight in the car on the way from the cemetery to the restaurant. It was a stupid argument, but we were all very upset. Jon was mad that Jessica didn't say anything at the grave site. He felt like it was dishonorable. I knew that Jessica had so many thoughts in her head all the time about Jonathan, but she was not talking so she wouldn't break down. I understood that, but we all weren't logical that day. Jon went to the restaurant and Jessica and I went to the Starbucks down the street and we refused to come to dinner until Jon apologized for freaking out in the car. Dinner was awful while we put a fake smile on our faces and pretended we were celebrating Jonathan's life. In reality we were mourning his death. A few people left us cards and flowers. That was so nice. It really helped me. Please remember your friends on this day. Send a thoughtful text. Bring them a cup of coffee. Please do something. I would describe that night as ugly, some twisted story from the Twilight Zone. You know like the man who found himself in a world by himself with endless time and an endless supply of book and then his glasses broke. Remember his anguish? Well, if you don't, look it up. It's a good one. That's the way I felt. That I had been given a perfect life, but then my son died and my glasses broke and I started to see my perfect life in distorted ways. The story would be, look at this lovely family eating dinner at this hip joint, but their glasses make them think they are eating with pigs. Or something like that.

I woke up the next morning and felt a little different. And the day after a little more different, like a weight had been lifted off my shoulder and my step got a little lighter and there was a little more love in my heart. I'm not sure why. It took me by surprise. It was such a small difference but I noticed it. If you carried around an hundred pound backpack for a year and then took off five pounds you would notice it. I think I had held that one year mark in my mind and I thought if I could make it that long, I could make it longer and there was some relief that I did. I had passed a milestone. I had made it one year. I was a survivor. I made it. I'm telling you I never thought I could. I never thought I could live without him. I never thought I could listen to music or laugh or look forward to growing old with my husband or having grandchildren. I did not think it was possible. For a person that could barely tolerate a minute of life without her son, one year was huge. In the beginning survival is one minute at a time. That is 525,600 minutes to live through and those minutes feel longer than an actual 60 seconds! I want to say to every single person that is living through grief that you can make the sad story better. You can.

We would go through many more trials and tribulations. The grieving process had only really just started. I would say after one year we made it through phase one. I'm not sure how many phases there are. I know the experts say there are five, but I think there are endless phases. Our next phase as we passed through the intense pain was just putting our lives back together, patching up neglected relationships, unpacking boxes, learning how to live again, that sort of stuff.

In one of my dreams I was an assistant to the President and I was inside working in the White House and you were playing on a swing set outside with some other worker's kids. I eventually went out to check on you. You were so much happier than I had ever seen you and you were getting along so well with the other kids. You jumped off the swing and said to me, "Do you mind if I stay here Mom? You go and work and take care of business. I'll be right here." And that was the last dream I had with Jonathan in it for a long time.

Dear Jonathan,

I forgive you. I know it was a mistake. I know that 12 year olds don't understand death and dying. I know you didn't know what you were really doing. You didn't mean to hurt us. You just weren't thinking. You gave us extraordinary signs, ones we could not dispute were coming from you. You've done your job here. Now go make world peace in between wake boarding sessions in heaven. I love you forever, every single day!

Mom

Dear Mom,

I'm smiling at you right now and I'm giving you a big hug! You are going to help me make world peace and put your suit on because you are going to go wake boarding too! Life is just one big adventure mom and it never ends! Stop worrying so much and start playing! I love you more, every single day!

Jonathan

When you died and I thought about living without you, it's like someone gave me a Swiss knife, a flashlight, and some Birkenstocks and said now you have to cross the Rocky mountains. Imagine that? How could you feed yourself, protect yourself, and hike those rugged mountains with sandals, a knife, and flashlight? That's how hard living without you is. Almost impossible. Yet I got up every morning after an almost sleepless night and I battled the day. Each day was as tiring as if I was climbing vertical walls of rock with my bare hands and as turbulent as the white waters without a paddle. Along the way, I met people and spirits and they handed me a thought, prayer, a hug, special tools to help me on my journey and finally the steps were easier. I confidently walked out of the Rocky mountains, my pack full and my spirit a little more peaceful and I felt like I really did something important. However, the trip isn't over. Upon my last step I was then told, my pack had been filled with tools, now I have to use them to cross the Sahara Desert. I understand now. This is a journey, not a destination.

EPILOGUE

It's now been 2.5 years. I'm still in the desert, but I have traveled so far. When I read over my first year I can hardly believe how devastated I was. I ended it at the first year because when Jonathan died I didn't think I could make it one day and a year seemed so impossibly far off. One year was my milestone. The changes I made in one year were about surviving. And you will too! The hard part for me was to remember to keep using the tools I was given. Keep doing good with your life. Dedicate yourself to actually making your dreams reality. Appreciate small things in life. Keep journaling and assess distorted thoughts. Be supportive to others grieving. Pray for guidance. I do believe I was guided to read certain books at certain times to help me through different stages. Keep moving. Rest if need be, but don't quit. Believe that he is waiting on the other side. As time has passed since the one year mark I really did learn to forgive and let go. The anger and blame I felt for others has been replaced by love. I was given the gift to tap into connecting with the other side and that knowing has given me a certain peace and confidence. Years later, my Dad passed and I had visions before and after he died and a dream with him and Jonathan in it. If there was any gift I could give you it would be faith in the afterlife. It does exist. Knowing that doesn't make all the pain go away, but it certainly helps. In the beginning you just have to get through the moments of the day. As time goes on, you can start focusing on your future and you start to see that life will go on. Good things will eventually happen to replace the bad. You do have to put in the work though. You have to show up on some days. You live in the present, but eventually you can even think about a future, a future without your loved one. I've started to put in place the components of a new career. I've been able to let go of some of my material fears. I used to think we needed to learn how to live as a family of three. I know now we will always be four. He is still with us. I now actually feel him as a presence in our lives instead of an idea. I now am able to just be. Breathing has become natural and not forced and I am comfortable in my own skin. The trick is to turn your loss into good things. We will all experience bad things in our lives but you can control how you feel about them. Sometimes how you control things comes naturally, other times it's a choice. Sometimes the gifts you receive from a loss are immediate, other times it's years later before you realize the good things that have happened because of a loss. I did realize that for myself healing was a conscious process. I don't know that time heals all wounds. Time does help, but you have to help time. I'm proud of how much we have grown as a family and that we were able to come together and help each other heal. I am still on this journey, learning and searching. I always will be, but life is good and I have hope for the future.

ACKNOWLEDGEMENTS

There were so many people in the background that helped me through my journey through grief and with the book, but here are the ones that I feel deserve special thanks. Thank you to my daughter for believing me and trusting that I actually saw the visions and allowing herself to heal through my visions. Thank you to my sister Paula for listening to all my stories and sharing her own with me. We spent hours upon hours discussing our signs and visions. Thank you Valerie for your concrete advise and counseling. Thank you Sally for reading my book and giving me the confidence to publish it. Thank you Victoria for helping me edit the book. Thank you Tanya for holding my business together while I was in the depths of despair. Thank you Susie for all the nights we sat by the fire and you kept me from falling into the abyss. Thank you Carrie for the amazing reading. Thank you to both Heather's for your messages and just being great friends. Thank you Brooke for sharing your visions with me so I didn't feel like I was going crazy. Thank you Megan for beginning the process. My life is so different now! Thank you Chad for your amazing sermons! I can't forget The Bad Ass Moms for their endless support. Thank you Anne Stafford for the amazing family photos at the park that are priceless beyond words. Thank you to the Davies family. You saved us so many times! Thank you Eric, for keeping things light. Thank you Mom for loving me and continuing to talk about Jonathan all the time, sharing memories. Thank you Jon for having faith in me and being my rock. Thank you Jonathan for being you and inspiring me from beyond. Thank you for all the messages, dreams, God wink's. Thank you for everything!

Made in the USA
San Bernardino, CA
20 April 2018